Attachment
Sociology and Social Worlds

Edited by Peter Redman

Manchester University Press
Manchester and New York
distributed exclusively in the USA by Palgrave
in association with

The Open University

This book is part of a series published by Manchester University Press in association with The Open University. The three books in the Sociology and Social Worlds series are:

Security: Sociology and Social Worlds (edited by Simon Carter, Tim Jordan and Sophie Watson)

Attachment: Sociology and Social Worlds (edited by Peter Redman)

Conduct: Sociology and Social Worlds (edited by Liz McFall, Paul du Gay and Simon Carter)

This publication forms part of the Open University course *Making social worlds* (DD308). Details of this and other Open University courses can be obtained from the Student Registration and Enquiry Service, The Open University, PO Box 197, Milton Keynes, MK7 6BJ, United Kingdom; tel. +44 (0)845 300 6090; email general-enquiries@open.ac.uk.

Alternatively, you may visit The Open University website at http://www.open.ac.uk where you can learn more about the wide range of courses and packs offered at all levels by The Open University.

To purchase a selection of Open University course materials visit http://www.ouw.co.uk, or contact Open University Worldwide Ltd, Walton Hall, Milton Keynes MK7 6AA, United Kingdom for a brochure, tel. +44 (0)1908 858785; fax +44 (0)1908 858787; email ouw-customer-services@open.ac.uk

Attachment

Sociology and Social Worlds

Manchester University Press
Oxford Road
Manchester M13 9NR, UK
and Room 400, 175 Fifth Avenue, New York, NY 10010, USA

www.manchesteruniversitypress.co.uk

First published 2008

A catalogue record of this book is available from the British Library

ISBN 978 0 7190 7812 5 *paperback*

Library of Congress Cataloguing-in-Publication Data

CIP data applied for

Edited and designed by The Open University.

Typeset in India by Alden Prepress Services, Chennai.

Printed and bound in the United Kingdon by TJ International Ltd, Padstow.

1.1

Contents

Notes on contributors

Jacqui Gabb is a Staff Tutor at The Open University. She is interested in developing interdisciplinary approaches for researching and theorising relationships, particularly in the areas of families and kin relationships, intimacy and sexuality, and, more generally, in exploring the potential of qualitative mixed-methods research. She has published widely in the area of sexuality and family relationships. She is the author of *Researching Intimacy and Sexuality in Families* (Macmillan, forthcoming).

Liz McFall is Lecturer in Sociology at The Open University. Her work is situated within the historical sociology of economic life with particular emphasis on the role of promotional practices in the 'making' of markets and consumers. She is the author of *Advertising: A Cultural Economy* (Sage, 2004) and a number of articles exploring nineteenth-century promotional culture, consumption and life assurance.

Fabian Muniesa is a researcher at the École des Mines de Paris, where he teaches economic sociology. His main research interest is in the social study of finance, an area in which he develops a perspective grounded in science and technology studies. He is the co-editor (with Donald MacKenzie and Lucia Siu) of *Do Economists Make Markets? On the Performativity of Economics* (Princeton, 2007).

Peter Redman is Senior Lecturer in Sociology at The Open University. His research includes work on gender and schooling, as well as psychoanalytically inflected approaches to social and cultural identity formation (including, with du Gay and Evans, the edited volume *Identity: A Reader*, Sage/ The Open University, 2000). He is currently working on a project exploring the historical formation of heterosexual masculinities in the immediate post-war period.

Michael Rustin is Professor of Sociology at the University of East London and a Visiting Professor at the Tavistock Clinic. He has been writing about psychoanalysis, and especially about its relation to social and cultural questions, for many years, and is internationally recognised as having played a leading role in the development of a psychoanalytically informed sociology. His books include *The Good Society and the Inner World* (Verso, 1991); *Narratives of Love and Loss* (with Margaret Rustin, 2nd edn, Karnac, 2001); *Reason and Unreason: Psychoanalysis, Science and Politics* (Continuum, 2001); *Mirror to Nature: Drama, Psychoanalysis and Society* (with Margaret Rustin, Karnac, 2002); and *Culture and the Unconscious* (ed. with Caroline Bainbridge et al., Palgrave, 2007).

Joanne Whitehouse-Hart is a researcher and Associate Lecturer at The Open University. She is currently working for a PhD on the emotional significance of 'favourite' film and television programmes, using a psycho-social audience research method.

Kath Woodward is Senior Lecturer in Sociology at The Open University and has particular research interests in gender identities, including feminist critiques of embodiment and social and cultural transformations. She has published widely on these matters, including *Understanding Identity* (Arnold, 2003), and more recently in the field of sport, *Boxing, Masculinity Identity: the 'I' of the Tiger* (Routledge, 2006) and the interdisciplinary book, *Social Sciences; the Big Issues* (Routledge, 2003). She is a member of the Open University Centre for Citizenship, Identities and Governance (CCIG), Identities strand and of the ESRC funded Centre of Research on Socio-Cultural Change (CRESC) based at Manchester and The Open University working on the diversity policies and transformations of racialised masculinities in sport. She is currently working on 'Sport Across Diasporas' as part of an AHRC Diasporas, Migration and Identities programme project on the BBC World Service.

Series preface

Sociology and Social Worlds is a series of three stand-alone books designed to explore the characteristics and benefits of sociological approaches to the social worlds in which we live. The books form the main study materials for the Open University course of the same name, *Making social worlds* (DD308), which aims to demonstrate the insights that sociology offers into everyday life, individual behaviour, the relationships between people and between people and things. The series considers how social worlds meet – and sometimes fail to meet – individual needs for security, attachment and order. Supported by examples ranging from Harry Potter to concentration camps, the books demonstrate that sociological approaches can help explain how individuals operate in the world, how social experience is shaped by nature and the material world, and how individual, social lives are made meaningful through culture and the media. The series takes account of the way in which sociology has been shaped by other disciplines and intellectual approaches, including cultural studies, media studies, history, psychology, anthropology and women's studies.

The first book in the series, *Security*, examines what security means in a variety of social and individual contexts. Authors consider issues ranging from geopolitical concerns such as global warming, terrorism and asylum seekers through to the intimate world of home and psychological development to help explain how security intersects with the making of social worlds. Through critical, sociological analyses of the character of material, natural, political and psychological 'threats' the authors show how security is constructed at different times and places.

The second book, *Attachment*, addresses attachment as a fundamental – and frequently overlooked – dimension of social life. Attachments between people, and between people and objects, make up the social worlds we inhabit. This book brings together a range of approaches (such as social constructionism, psychoanalysis and the anthropology of material culture) to investigate how the processes of attachment and detachment occur. Exploring a number of areas – including the nature of attachment to characters and plotlines in reality television shows, intimacy in parent–child relationships, and sport and the masculine body – the book offers a clear and accessible introduction to attachment as an issue of sociological concern.

Conduct, the final book in the series, offers an innovative perspective on how individual behaviour is ordered in social worlds. It aims to show that matters of conduct – habits, attributes, capacities, manners, skills and behaviours – and the norms, techniques, laws and rules which regulate them, offer a crucial means through which sociologists can understand how social worlds are put together, change and break apart. Topics including self-service shopping, personal finance, violence and drunkenness are used as part of a sustained analysis of the close links between individual conduct and particular social worlds.

Open University courses are produced by course teams. These teams involve authors from The Open University as well as other institutions, course and project managers, tutors, external assessors, editors, designers, audio and video producers, administrators and secretaries. Academics on the *Making social worlds* course team were based mainly in the Sociology department within The Open University's Faculty of Social Sciences, but the course team also drew upon the expertise of colleagues in the Economic and Social Research Council (ESRC) Centre for Research on Socio-cultural Change (CRESC) and from other universities and institutions in order to construct a course with interdisciplinary foundations and appeal. While book editors have primary responsibility for the content of each book, the assignment of editors' names to books does not adequately convey the collective nature of production at The Open University. I'd like to thank all my colleagues on the course team for their intellectual energy, hard work and unfailing good humour. Particular thanks are due to Lucy Morris, who has, among many other things, been a resourceful, professional and efficient Course Manager.

Liz McFall, Course Chair

On behalf of the *Making social worlds* course team

Introduction

Peter Redman

Contents

1   Attachment and social worlds

In Chapter 4 of this book (see Section 5) Fabian Muniesa quotes from the opening scene of Francis Ford Coppolla's celebrated film, *The Godfather* (Paramount, 1972). Amerigo Bonasera stands before mafia boss, Don Corleone – the Godfather of the film's title – pleading with him to take revenge against two young men who have beaten and attempted to rape his daughter. The Godfather appears reluctant. 'Why did you go to the police?', he says, 'Why didn't you come to me first?'. Increasingly desperate, Bonasera offers the Godfather money, 'How much shall I pay you?', he asks. Don Corleone does not want his money, however. Instead, he offers Bonasera his 'friendship'. He will do what Bonasera asks if, in return, Bonasera gives him homage and allegiance. Bonasera acquiesces, kissing Don Corleone's hand and calling him 'Godfather'. 'Good', Don Corleone says, 'Someday, and that day may never come, I'll call upon you to do a service for me.'

Muniesa reads this exchange as a struggle over two very different types of attachment. Bonasera wishes to connect himself to the Godfather via the conventions of a straightforward financial transaction. Don Corleone will perform a service for him (albeit one that is violent and illegal); Bonasera will pay for this service; after which they will have no further obligations towards each other. Don Corleone, on the other hand, insists that the attachment takes a form closer to that of feudal vassalage. He will perform the service Bonasera has requested as a 'gift' but, henceforth, Bonasera will be in his debt. Should the time come to return the Godfather's favour, Bonasera will be a servant bound to do his master's bidding.

This reading of the opening scene of *The Godfather* provides a powerful introduction to the central theme of *Attachment: Sociology and Social Worlds*. Attachment, in the sense used in this volume, can be thought of as referring to the diverse ways in which ongoing connections of varying kinds are forged between people and between people and things. Such connections are important because, in making these, we make and remake the very fabric of our social worlds – a term that can be understood as referring to 'a unit or set of social interactions that is not confined by geography or formal membership of organisations or institutions, but rather is an assemblage or association with shared commitments or practices' (Carter et al., 2008, Introduction, Section 1). Attachments (and detachments) are, in this view, the means by which people and objects are assembled into the regular, patterned and relatively stable arrangements that make up the social landscape. They are the basis of social connectedness: what makes social worlds hang together and keeps them going on.

Figure 1
Bonasera asks Don
Corleone to avenge the
assault on his daughter

An important implication of this claim is that the specificities of a social world arise, in part, from the types of attachments or connections that constitute it. Put simply, different forms of connection make different kinds of social world. This is all too apparent in *The Godfather* example. As Muniesa argues, the form of attachment upon which Don Corleone insists – one based on the mutual obligations and close personal ties of vassalage – produces a world that is corrupt, insecure and murderous. Although he is himself soliciting violence, Bonasera tries to avoid becoming entangled in this world by making a different kind of connection to it. His hope is that, if he pays for Don Corleone's services, his attachment to him will be temporary – that, having paid, he will be able to detach himself from any obligation to the Godfather and return to the law-abiding world of mainstream American society. However, as Bonasera discovers, Don Corleone's world is one in which detachment mechanisms of this kind are absent. To attach oneself to the world of the Godfather is to become permanently entangled within it. (Bonasera perhaps gets off lightly when, asked to return the Godfather's favour later in the film, his task is merely to make presentable the bullet-riddled corpse of Don Corleone's son.)

2   Attachment theory and sociology

Although processes of attachment and detachment can be seen as significant mechanisms by which social worlds are made, the terms themselves are not part of the mainstream of sociological debate. This is not to say that the question of social connectedness and its failure has been absent from sociological enquiry. Indeed, as Michael Rustin writes in Chapter 5 of this volume (see Section 2), 'Explaining the preconditions for social connectedness and social order has been a central issue – perhaps *the* central issue – for sociology'. As Rustin explains, classical sociology was preoccupied with the question of how existing social worlds were 'to hold together' as 'the bonds of religion, tradition, community and kinship weakened' in the face of the growing 'individualism, greater mobility, market exchange, industrialisation and urbanisation' of the modern world. However, if social connectedness has been a matter of significant concern for sociologists, it has not always been thought of in terms of processes of attachment. Indeed, as Chapter 1 in this volume notes, as a concept, attachment has been more closely associated with the discipline of psychology, in particular the attachment theory of the celebrated British psychologist, John Bowlby (1969, 1973, 1980) and his followers (see, for example, Ainsworth, 1982; Ainsworth et al., 1978; Main et al., 1985).

Attachment theory is based on the premise that human infants have an inherent propensity to forge strong psychological and emotional bonds with their primary carers. As the psychiatrist Jeremy Holmes has written, these experiences of psychological attachment in early childhood are then said to form 'internal working models' that profoundly influence our subsequent sense of ourselves and the quality of the relationships we form in later life. He writes:

> The developing child builds up a set of models of the self and others, based on repeated patterns of interactive experience. These 'basic assumptions' ... form relatively fixed representational models which the child uses to predict and relate to the world. A securely attached child will store an internal working model of a responsive, loving, reliable care-giver, and of a self that is worthy of love and attention and will bring these assumptions to bear on all other relationships. Conversely, an insecurely attached child may view the world as a dangerous place in which other people are to be treated with great caution, and see himself as ineffective and unworthy of love. These assumptions are relatively stable and enduring.
>
> (Holmes, 1993, pp. 78–9)

As this implies, attachment theory has potentially important implications for the making of social worlds. In particular, it predicts that, if all goes reasonably well in their lives, individuals who were securely attached to their primary carer in early childhood will be more likely than their peers to be endowed with capacities that may, for example, help them do better at school; be more creative, self-confident and independent; and form more stable and fulfilling relationships. Indeed, there is now a large body of evidence from longitudinal studies suggesting a strong relationship between the attachment styles of early childhood and later developments of this kind (see, for instance, Steele, 2003, pp. 97–102). Moreover, if early experiences of psychological attachment have consequences for society, there are also grounds for believing that social conditions have consequences for early experiences of attachment. As Holmes (1993, p. 204) has argued, insecure social conditions produce insecure adults who are, in consequence, less able to provide the sort of care that promotes securely attached infants. Drawing out some of the social and political implications of these ideas, he writes:

> a psychologically-informed politics would include among its basic principles respect for persons, the capacity to listen, acknowledgement of pain, acceptance of the need for legitimate expressions of anger and, above all, the provision of a secure base for all its citizens as a precondition for exploration and growth.
>
> (Holmes, 1996, p. 40)

As this suggests, for attachment theory, security is central to human experience and well-being, not only in infancy but throughout life. Infants thrive in conditions of secure psychological attachment; individuals and societies thrive – are at their most dynamic and creative – when social relations and institutions are not only stable, ordered and secure but also respectful and attentive to people's needs.

However, while attachment theory clearly has much to teach sociology, it is not, from a sociological point of view, the only or, necessarily, the most useful tool with which to study the connections that are forged between people and between people and things. This is because the forms of connectedness with which attachment theory deals are very specific: primarily, those related to the psychological and emotional experience of security in infancy and the consequences of this for the individual's sense of self and the interpersonal relationships he or she makes in later life. Although important, these attachments clearly encompass only a limited range of the myriad and heterogeneous forms of social connection (and disconnection) from which the fabric of the social world is made. Whatever the advantages of attachment theory, sociological enquiry clearly needs to range more widely if this heterogeneity is to be addressed.

3   Attachment in a sociological perspective: 'orientations' and 'concerns'

As will be discussed further below (see Sections 4 and 5), the chapters that make up this volume draw on a diverse and sometimes competing range of theoretical resources. However, despite these differences in approach, we can discern within them a number of common *orientations* and an interest in a range of specifically sociological *concerns*. The former derive from two of the more familiar meanings that attachment has in the English language. For instance, among a number of definitions offered by the *Oxford English Dictionary (OED),* attachment is identified as referring to, 'The fact or condition of being fastened on or to' (as in the phrase, 'the trailer was attached to the car'). In this light, we can say that, understood sociologically, attachment can be thought of, in the first instance, as referring to the *practical mechanisms* by which people, and people and objects, get connected to each other.

However, the *OED* goes on to describe attachment as referring to, 'The fact or condition of being attached by sympathy; affection, devotion, fidelity'. This meaning is captured in a phrase such as, 'the members of the family were much attached to each other'. In the light of this second definition, we can say that attachment can also refer to the means by which people and objects are brought emotionally to life and become personally meaningful. In other words, understood sociologically, attachment can also be said to refer to a sense of *emotional investment*.

Figure 2
Attachment can be thought of as referring to the practical mechanisms by which people, and people and things are connected

Figure 3
Attachment can also be thought of as referring to the processes by which people develop emotional investments in other people and things

These two orientations towards attachment – attachment as a practical mechanism and as emotional investment – provide something of an organising device for the chapters that make up this volume, with Chapters 1, 3 and 4 being primarily orientated towards the investigation of the practical mechanisms by which attachments are forged and Chapters 2 and 5 being primarily orientated towards questions of emotional investment.

A second strand that can be said to run through the various chapters that make up *Attachment: Sociology and Social Worlds* relates to the fact that, to varying degrees, they address the sociological 'concerns' of mediation, matter and the individual. While these in no sense exhaust the range of concerns with which sociological enquiry deals, each can be thought of as indexing a substantive area of current debate within sociology and the social sciences more generally. In their discussion of the concerns, **Carter et al. (2008, Introduction, Section 2.1)** explain that 'mediation' can be understood as drawing our attention to two issues in particular: first, the media and their role in the making of social worlds; and, second, the concept of translation. As Stuart Hall (1997, p. 209) has written, the media (understood as the main means of mass communication, including the internet, television, film, radio and print) now 'form a critical part of the material infrastructure of modern societies and are the principal means by which ideas and images are circulated'. As such, the media undoubtedly warrant serious sociological consideration, a fact reflected in a number of the chapters in *Attachment: Sociology and Social Worlds*, but most particularly in Chapter 2's focus on people's emotional attachments to media texts.

Although mediation understood in this first sense is clearly important, it is its second sense – that of translation – that is arguably most central to this volume. **Carter et al. (2008, Introduction, Section 2.1)** describe translation as referring to 'those processes that allow statements or artefacts to pass from one social world into another', offering as an example of this the way in which the passport 'translates' a particular individual into a document that allows him or her to be recognised by nation states. From the point of view of attachment, this draws our attention to the *medium* through which one thing – whether a person or an object – is connected to another, and to the *transformative work* this medium performs on the people and objects in question. To take only one example, Chapter 4 in this volume is particularly interested in the material devices (for instance, cash and receipts) by which processes of economic attachment and detachment are achieved. Such devices can be thought of as the medium through which these processes work and, in consequence, as mediating (and thereby changing) the relationships involved. Thus, for example, a cash payment made when purchasing a good in a shop will briefly attach two previously unconnected people – the buyer and the seller – in a relationship of mutual obligation (the seller must hand over the good to the buyer). The provision of a receipt, proving that the seller has handed over the good and been paid for it, will then detach the buyer from the seller, leaving them 'quits' or without ongoing mutual obligations.

If mediation refers both to translation and the role of the media in contemporary social life, 'matter' is identified by **Carter et al. (2008, Introduction, Section 2.2)** as referring, principally, to the role material objects play in the making of social worlds. For instance, in the example used in the previous paragraph, it is noticeable that the process of attachment and detachment described is achieved via material objects (cash and a paper receipt). Without these, it would be very difficult for the economic relationship involved to function. As **Carter et al (2008, Introduction, Section 2.2)** go on to suggest, this in turn raises questions about the exact relationship between the material and social worlds: are they distinct; related hierarchically (with one 'constructing' or otherwise determining the other); or mutually constitutive? These are issues central to a number of the chapters in this volume and they will be discussed in more detail in Section 4 of this Introduction.

Finally, the 'individual' refers us to a long tradition of sociological debate over the nature of the relationship between the individual and the social. As **Carter et al. (2008, Introduction, Section 2.3)** explain, it is fair to say that sociologists tend to view individuals as being in some way shaped and influenced by the social worlds they inhabit. This relationship is sometimes viewed as one in which the social world imposes itself on individuals, enabling or, more often than not, constraining what the individual in question is or is not able to be or do. As is argued by **du Gay et al. (2008, Introduction),** the problem with such a formulation is that it tends to construct the individual and the social as distinct and separate entities. In contrast, it may be better to think of the relationship between the individual and the social as one of mutual constitution. From this point of view, individuals do not precede social worlds and social worlds do not precede individuals. Instead, each exists only in and through the other. If this proposition is accepted, the question for sociological debate is not so much *whether* individuals and social worlds are related but *how* and the consequentiality that should be accorded to each. Another way to put this would be to ask, in what ways and to what extent (if any) can we say that individuals have attributes and capacities which, even if formed in relation to the social, nevertheless enable and constrain social possibilities?

While these sociological concerns can be said to run through the chapters that make up *Attachment: Sociology and Social Worlds*, this does not mean that they are addressed systematically by each chapter in turn.

instead, individual chapters tend to focus on only two of the three, and their depth of engagement with these varies depending on their relevance to the issues in hand. Nevertheless, as with the two 'orientations' discussed earlier in this section, the concerns provide an organising device for the book as a whole. Some of the issues they raise are explored in the next two sections but they are also returned to in chapter conclusions and they provide the major focus of discussion in the book's Afterword.

4 Structure of the book (i): the practical mechanisms of attachment and detachment

As indicated in the preceding section, although informed by rather different theoretical traditions, Chapters 1, 3 and 4 each emphasise the practical mechanisms by which social attachments can be said to be forged. In Chapter 1, by Jacqui Gabb, these mechanisms are approached from a feminist social constructionist perspective. As Gabb explains in the introduction to her chapter, the various strands that make up social constructionism can be characterised as sharing a central preoccupation with the role of social meanings and practices in the making of social worlds. In other words, social constructionists are interested in what people do when they interact with each other and in the collective social meanings that can be said to organise these interactions. This social constructionist approach is deployed in the chapter to argue that parents' attachments to their children are not given in nature but are instead mediated by social meanings and practices. As this implies, for social constructionism, social practice is understood primarily as existing in relation to an 'underlying' repertoire of collective social meanings which, although not determining how any given social practice is enacted, nevertheless provides the vocabulary and the rules for its enactment. This is apparent, for example, in Chapter 1's discussion of Arlie Hochschild's (2003) notion of 'feeling rules': the more or less loosely defined collective social codes that are said to regulate and direct what it is appropriate to feel in a given context.

The insights generated by social constructionist approaches are clearly of immense value. However, from the point of view of the arguments developed in Chapters 3 and 4, it is doubtful whether social constructionism provides us with the final word on social attachment and detachment. In particular, as Kath Woodward argues in Chapter 3, there may be a danger within social constructionist accounts that the *materiality* of the social world is collapsed into, and becomes little more than an effect of, social meaning and practice. This point can be illustrated in relation to the concept of 'materialisation' as used by the feminist philosopher and social theorist, Judith Butler (1993). As Gabb explains in Chapter 1 (see Section 3), in using the term materialisation Butler refers to the ways in which things which we might generally consider to have a material existence, independent of social meanings – such as biological sex – can, in fact, be thought of as brought into existence ('materialised') by these meanings and the social practices through which these meanings are given expression. For example, biological sex – understood as something that is *ascribed* to people rather than as something that is, in any straightforward sense, *inherent* in them – is said to be materialised through both the classificatory system of a two-sex model and specific social practices. Butler's famous example of this process of ascription is the midwife's cry, 'It's a girl!', which she describes as being less the reflection of a category given in nature (i.e. biological femaleness) than an instance of an ongoing practice of 'girling' by which biological femaleness is attributed to individuals possessing a particular type of body (Butler, 1993, p. 232).

From a sociological point of view, materialisation is, as a concept, undoubtedly productive. It not only confronts us with the extent to which our view of the world is mediated by available social meanings, but also demands that we attend to the ways in which these meanings take on a material existence as they are enacted within social practices. When inspected through the lens of materialisation, even the distinction between male and female is revealed to be as much a product of the codes of meaning circulating in contemporary Western societies as it is a result of variations found in nature. However, although Butler acknowledges the reality of a material world that exists beyond the boundaries of social meanings and practices, it is possible to argue that she accords this world very little consequentiality (see, for instance, Butler, 1993, pp. 8–13). In particular, there is relatively little sense in her argument of the possibility that social meanings and practices are themselves mediated – that is, *enabled* and *constrained* – by the obdurate materiality of human bodies and non-human objects (Reckwitz, 2002).

In Chapter 3, Kath Woodward takes up this point in relation to the materiality of the human body. Focusing on boxing, the chapter asks how it is that boxers become attached to an activity (hitting and being hit) that is inherently painful and dangerous. Woodward answers this question by reference to the notion of embodiment and, in particular, the concept of 'body-reflexive practices' (Connell, 1995, pp. 46–66). As Woodward explains, Connell is critical of both social constructionist accounts of the body and what she calls 'sociobiological' approaches. The former, Connell argues, all but write the body out of existence, assuming that bodies are little more than the bearers of whatever social meaning happens to be applied to them (as is perhaps the case with

Butler's example of the midwife's cry, 'It's a girl!'). Sociobiological approaches, on the other hand, all but write social meanings and practices out of existence. For sociobiology, social meanings and practices are assumed either to be determined by biology (for example, the claim that women are 'naturally' fitted for childcare by virtue of being biologically female) or are assumed to be relatively minor cultural elaborations of a more fundamental and significant biological 'base'. Connell rejects both social constructionist and sociobiological options, arguing instead that the social and the body are inextricably entwined. Bodily properties and capacities are lived and take on meaning, she suggests, only *within* social practices that actively shape and mould the bodies upon which they work. Thus, the practices and techniques of the boxer's craft are, literally, 'made flesh' – written into the way he moves in the ring; the sequencing and speed of the punches he throws; and his body's ability to endure physical assault. At the same time, however, social practices are themselves shaped, limited and given meaning by properties and capacities that are *inherent* to the body. As the boxer ages, for example, the skill and speed with which he can throw punches will decline, no matter how rigorous his training. From this point of view, then, the body and the social are always entwined. In effect, as Woodward argues in Chapter 3, the body is always present in and mediated by the social and the social is always present in and mediated by the materiality of the body.

If Chapter 3 draws our attention to the material body's presence in and mediation of processes of attachment and detachment, Chapter 4, by Fabian Muniesa, underlines the role of non-human 'things' – objects, artefacts and technical apparatuses – in these processes. As its Introduction identifies, although focusing on the sociology of economic life, the chapter utilises approaches first developed in other fields of enquiry. In particular, it draws on actor-network theory (ANT), and the anthropology of material culture (see, for instance, Latour, 1987; Miller, 2005). Muniesa argues that these approaches are useful in studying processes of attachment and detachment in economic life because they view things as playing a central role in the making of social worlds.

As its name suggests, the anthropology of material culture studies material artefacts and environments (whether ox ploughs, mantelpiece ornaments, denim jeans, airports, or anything else made or adapted by people). Material artefacts and environments are interesting because they can be said to carry or embody social meaning and, in so doing, *constitute* social worlds. For example, in Section 4 of Chapter 4, Muniesa cites the work of the economic sociologist Viviana Zelizer (2005) who has documented legal disputes over payments received in the context of sexual relations. In one case, two sisters were accused of non-payment of taxes on money received for what the prosecution defined as prostitution. The women were cleared of the charges on appeal, in part because they were able to show that the payments from the man in question were accompanied by love letters. In effect, the court decided the payments were gifts rather than income and that, in consequence, no income tax was due to be paid on them.

As Muniesa suggests, this example is interesting because it exposes the central role played by material artefacts in mediating the meaning of an act – in this instance an act attaching three people in a particular form of economic relationship. The meaning of the act, Muniesa argues, resided less in what the sisters' lover *did* (that is, making payments to the sisters) than in the material *artefacts* through which the act was transacted (for example, cheques plus love letters). Despite its slightly unconventional nature, the act became a gift (rather than a payment for sexual services) precisely because the payments were accompanied by material artefacts of a particular kind: letters of affection (much as a gift of money on a birthday will often be accompanied by a card). The important point here is that these material artefacts were central in *constituting* the act's meaning. From this perspective, then, social worlds are made not only by what people do and what they mean when they do it (as social constructionism tends to argue) but also by material artefacts and environments and what these mean.

This example clearly establishes the potential importance of things as a constituent element of the mechanisms by which attachments are forged in economic life. However, as the previous section of this Introduction suggested, material artefacts are important not only because they help constitute social meaning but because their materiality itself matters. This is an issue of central importance to the second approach upon which Muniesa draws, ANT. Outlining the principles of ANT, **Simon Carter and George Davey Smith (2008, Section 5)** explain that ANT rejects the social constructionist premise that society is constructed solely through human action and meaning and, instead, views social worlds as the outcome of various mechanisms by which, not only people, but also people and things are connected or assembled into specific relations or networks that are multiple, diverse and persist over time. Importantly, in studying these networks, ANT emphasises the fact that things have agency as much as people. In other words, things make things happen. In accounting for this non-human agency, ANT accords a central role to matter. We can illustrate this point by returning to the example, cited in the previous section, of the individual purchasing a good from a shop. As was suggested in relation to this example, without the materiality of the objects involved (that is, the cash used to buy the good and the receipt given in exchange for it), the transaction would be all but impossible. Imagine, for example, the chaos that would ensue if each buyer had to carry gold bullion and each seller had to keep a mental record of every item sold. In fact, all but the most straightforward of market transactions simply could not function without a portable means of payment (cash, debit cards, money transfers and so forth), and without an efficient means of permanently recording sales. As this suggests, things help constitute social worlds not only because, in a given context, they are ascribed with or 'carry' particular social meanings but because their material properties enable and constrain the horizon of the possible.

This argument might be taken to imply that the material world is somehow more fundamental than the social (in much the same way that, for sociobiology, the social is little more than an epiphenomenon of a more fundamental biological base). However, as Chapter 4 demonstrates, actor-network theorists characteristically suggest that the social and material worlds cannot be meaningfully separated. In this sense, although very different from Connell's account of body-reflexive practices, ANT offers a parallel perspective to it. For actor-network theorists, the social and the material exist in a relation of hybridity. Objects, they argue, are never purely material and the social is never purely social. Instead, we should think of the social as being present in and mediated by the material and the material as being present in and mediated by the social.

5   Structure of the book (ii): attachment as emotional investment

As the preceding section has detailed, one of the most obvious and productive ways in which to approach attachment from a sociological point of view is via the investigation of the various practical mechanisms by which, in different contexts, people are connected to other people and to things. Of course, such an approach need not preclude the study of emotional investment, the second form of attachment identified in Section 3 of this Introduction. As Chapter 1 in this volume suggests, emotional investments can, at the very least, be viewed as enabled and constrained by available social meanings and practices and can perhaps be seen as arising from these. However, it is possible to argue that it is in psychoanalytically informed accounts that emotional investment has been most systematically addressed. Psychoanalysis, as Section 3 of Chapter 2 argues, has at its heart the claim that there is an emotion-laden register of human experience (often referred to as an 'inner world' or 'inner reality'), primarily unconscious in character, which mediates our conscious experience of people and things in the external world. The primary mechanism by which this is said to occur is that of unconscious 'transference': the investing of the external world with thoughts and feelings derived from the inner world.

As this indicates, in contrast to approaches like that adopted in Chapter 1, psychoanalytically informed accounts view emotion (in the form of emotion-laden unconscious experience) not as something that is secondary to or even derived from social meaning and practices but as profoundly active and consequential in its own right. Emotion-laden unconscious processes are, in this view, integral to social processes of attachment and detachment: shaped by them but also shaping them and bringing them subjectively to life.

Chapter 2, by Peter Redman and Joanne Whitehouse-Hart, investigates this argument in the context of people's emotional attachments to media texts. The chapter focuses on research data drawn from the authors' viewing of the UK version of the reality television show *Big Brother,* in particular an extract from the research diary Peter Redman kept while watching the series. As might be expected from a conventional sociological analysis, the data show Redman actively 'reading' *Big Brother* via the collective social meanings available to him. However, the chapter suggests that the way in which these meanings were drawn upon in the moment-by-moment activity of viewing was highly selective, with issues related to age and masculinity to the fore. Furthermore, the authors argue that, when these issues appear in the data, they are saturated with anxiety. They interpret this anxiety, together with the selective nature of the cultural resources that were drawn upon, as evidence of unconscious transference. As he watched the show, they suggest, Redman's unconscious was actively mediating the ways in which he 'read' it, animating some dimensions of the interpretive resources available to him rather than others, and lending his use of these a specific emotional tone, colour and texture.

These arguments are taken up by Rustin in the book's final chapter which investigates in some detail how unconscious processes come to be present in and, thereby, help constitute relations within and between social institutions and groups. In particular, the chapter explores instances in which these relations – themselves forms of social connection and attachment – fail or break down. In so doing, Rustin draws on a number of psychoanalytic ideas, in particular: unconscious anxiety and the so-called 'paranoid-schizoid' defences against this; and problems with 'thinking' and the 'borderline' or 'narcissistic' states that are said to accompany these.

As the chapter explains, the notion of the paranoid-schizoid position was first developed in the work of Melanie Klein (1986 [1946]). It refers to a state of mind, said to be characteristic of early infancy, dominated by imagined threats to the self. The baby, Klein argued, is inevitably subject to a range of contradictory sensations and feelings and, at this early stage in its development, the mind is said to manage or mediate these contradictory experiences by appropriating the 'good' ones to itself and, in unconscious fantasy, splitting off and projecting the 'bad' ones onto the external world. As the chapter explains, this leads to a state of mind dominated by simple polarities (all that is 'me' is good; all that is 'not-me' is bad) and by persecutory anxieties (the sense that what is me and good is under constant threat from without). Although this state of mind is, we are told, particularly characteristic of early infancy, it is also described as a 'position' or unconscious configuration that persists throughout life – something which, to a greater or lesser extent, we all move in and out of on a daily basis. This is important because it allows Rustin to apply the notions of paranoid splitting and projection to the social life of institutions; to relations between ethnic groups; and even those between nation-states.

Rustin's exploration of his second group of concepts – problems with 'thinking' and the 'borderline' or 'narcissistic' states that are said to accompany this – starts with the work of the British psychoanalyst, Wilfred Bion. As Rustin explains, for Bion, 'thinking' refers to the capacity – partly conscious, partly unconscious – to acknowledge and process emotional experience (Bion, 1963). An individual who has been able to develop the capacity for such 'thought' is, Bion argues, better able to experience emotional complexity and to tolerate emotional states that are difficult or contradictory. As Rustin goes on to explain, one characteristic of so-called 'borderline' or 'narcissistic' states of mind is the refusal to do 'thinking' of this kind. The individual displaying such a state of mind is not so much unaware of an emotional reality as in retreat from it. The reality is disavowed, perhaps because it feels too painful to bear. Drawing on the work of Margaret Rustin, a child psychotherapist at London's Tavistock Clinic, Rustin applies these concepts to the case of Victoria Climbié, an eight-year-old child, known to her local social services department, who died while in her aunt's foster care. The social services department's failure to prevent Victoria Climbié's death was not, Rustin argues, simply a failure of procedure but reflected an inability to 'think' at an institutional level. In common with the other examples Rustin explores in Chapter 5, this once again suggests that unconscious processes are not simply restricted to individuals but also characterise relations within and between organisations and social groups. An understanding of how these processes work – that is, how the unconscious mediates the collective life of organisations and social groups – is, Rustin argues, crucial to our understanding of why social attachments sometimes fail.

As the Afterword to this volume will argue in more detail, the presence of psychoanalytic arguments in *Attachment: Sociology and Social Worlds* throws a particularly strong light on debates over the relationship between the individual and the social. Earlier in this Introduction (see

Section 3), it was suggested that the question that needs to be asked of this relationship is not *whether* the individual and the social are related but *how* and the degree of consequentiality that should be accorded to each. As the preceding paragraphs indicate, psychoanalytic accounts – focusing as they do on processes of unconscious fantasy and transference – inevitably emphasise capacities that can be said to be inherent to the individual. However, this does not mean that arguments informed by psychoanalysis view the individual as preceding the social. As the conclusion to Chapter 2 explains, while unconscious transference is inescapably individual, it is also deeply marked by the social worlds of which it is a part. This is because the people and objects animated by unconscious transference are, in turn, said to be internalised or 'introjected', a process which modifies the terrain of the inner world. From this perspective, the social mediates and is thus constitutive of the unconscious even as the unconscious mediates and is constitutive of the social. Nevertheless, while psychoanalytic approaches – in common with the arguments advanced in Chapters 1, 3 and 4 – view the social and the individual as mutually constitutive, it remains the case that, compared with these other arguments, they view the individual in more normative terms. Not only do psychoanalytic approaches contain a well-developed sense of what constitutes human well-being, they also view human experience as having a quite high degree of continuity across time and place, a position with which (as the Afterword to this volume will explore in more detail) the arguments advanced in Chapters 1, 3 and 4 tend strongly to disagree. In consequence, just as Chapters 1, 3 and 4 can be seen as being engaged in a dialogue over the status of matter, Chapters 2 and 5 can be viewed as being in dialogue with the other chapters in the book over the status of the individual.

In addressing these and other issues raised in this Introduction, *Attachment: Sociology and Social Worlds* does not seek to develop a particular 'line'. Still less does it seek to achieve a synthesis out of what are undoubtedly incommensurable positions. In setting out these various approaches, it is for the reader to decide which is the most useful for advancing our understanding of processes of attachment and detachment and the roles these play in the making of social worlds.

References

Ainsworth, M. (1982) 'Attachment: retrospect and prospect' in Parkes, C.M. and Stevenson-Hinde, J. (eds) *The Place of Attachment in Human Behaviour*, London, Tavistock.

Ainsworth, M., Blehar, M., Waters, E. and Wall, S. (1978) *Patterns of Attachment: Assessed in the Strange Situation at Home*, Hillsdale, NJ, Erlbaum.

Bion, W. (1963) *Learning from Experience*, London, Heinemann.

Bowlby, J. (1969) *Attachment*, London, Hogarth Press.

Bowlby, J. (1973) *Separation: Anxiety and Anger*, London, Hogarth Press.

Bowlby, J. (1980) *Loss: Sadness and Depression*, London, Hogarth Press.

Butler, J. (1993) *Bodies That Matter: On the Discursive Limits of Sex*, London, Routledge.

Carter, S. and Davey Smith, G. (2008) 'Health and security' in Carter, Jordan and Watson (eds) (2008).

Carter, S., Jordan, T. and Watson, S. (2008) 'Introduction' in Carter, Jordan and Watson (eds) (2008).

Carter, S., Jordan, T. and Watson, S. (eds) (2008) *Security: Sociology and Social Worlds*, Manchester, Manchester University Press/Milton Keynes, The Open University (Book 1 in this series).

Connell, R.W. (1995) *Masculinities*, Cambridge, Polity.

du Gay, P., McFall, L. and Carter, S. (2008) 'Introduction' in McFall, L., du Gay, P. and Carter, S. (eds) *Conduct: Sociology and Social Worlds*, Manchester, Manchester University Press/Milton Keynes, The Open University (Book 3 in this series).

Hall, S. (1997) 'The centrality of culture: notes on the cultural revolutions of our time' in Thompson, K. (ed.) *Media and Cultural Regulation*, London, Sage Publications/Milton Keynes, The Open University.

Hochschild, A.R. (2003) *The Commercialization of Intimate Life: Notes from Home and Work*, Berkeley, CA, University of California Press.

Holmes, J. (1993) *John Bowlby and Attachment Theory*, London, Routledge.

Holmes, J. (1996) 'Attachment theory and society' in Roberts, J. and Kraemer, S. (eds) *The Politics of Attachment: Towards a Secure Society*, London, Free Association Books.

Klein, M. (1986 [1946]) 'Notes on some schizoid mechanisms' in Mitchell, J. (ed.) *The Selected Melanie Klein*, Harmondsworth, Peregrine/Penguin.

Latour, B. (1987) *Science in Action: How to Follow Scientists and Engineers Through Society*, Milton Keynes, Open University Press.

Main, M., Kaplan, N. and Cassidy, J. (1985) 'Security in infancy, childhood, and adulthood: a move to the level of representation' in Bretherton, I. and Waters, E. (eds) 'Growing points of attachment theory and research', *Monographs of the Society for Research in Child Development*, vol. 50, nos 1–2, pp. 66–104.

Miller, D. (ed.) (2005) *Materiality*, Durham, NC, Duke University Press.

Reckwitz, A. (2002) 'The status of the "material" in theories of culture: from "social structure" to "artefacts"', *Journal for the Theory of Social Behaviour*, vol. 32, no. 2, pp. 195–216.

Steele, M. (2003) 'Attachment, actual experience and mental representation' in Green, V. (ed.) *Emotional Development in Psychoanalysis, Attachment Theory and Neuroscience: Creating Connections*, Hove, Brunner-Routledge.

The Godfather, film, directed by Francis Ford Coppola. USA: Paramount Pictures, 1972.

Zelizer, V.A. (2005) *The Purchase of Intimacy*, Princeton, NJ, Princeton University Press.

Chapter 1
Affective attachment in families

Jacqui Gabb

Contents

1 Introduction

> *Ann:*   *Everything, every, I think emotionally everything [is] related to Ollie*
> *from, you know, the moment he was conceived to being pregnant to*
> *being born, to being, every day of his life is a huge emotional thing*
> *for me ... I mean if anything happened to Ollie I just can't imagine*
> *what I'd feel like. It's like I mean the pleasure he gives both of us is*
> *unbelievable, you know ... Ollie's the most important thing in the*
> *world and that's it and we agree on that.*

This extract, like subsequent research data extracts in this chapter, is taken from the Economic and Social Research Council (ESRC)-funded study *Behind Closed Doors*. Ann, a 40-year-old mother, is describing the intensity of her feelings for her son, Ollie. It is the sort of comment that you may have heard many times before or it may be that you have experienced such emotions yourself. In this chapter we begin to explore the social context of these feelings – the way that parent – child attachments are understood as something special and different from all other relationships, forming the affective base of families. In emphasising social context in this manner, the chapter does not seek to deny the authenticity of parental feelings nor does it devalue the intensity of parent – child attachments. However, it argues that this intensity is not, as we might usually think, a straightforward feature of nature – something pre-programmed in our genes – but is, instead, a 'social construct'. This implies that parents' emotional investments in their children are, in some sense, taught and learned, reliant on normative understandings which emerge through mediated and culturally specific notions of 'good parenting'. For example, as you will see later in the chapter, it is possible to argue that such things as childcare handbooks, television programmes and professional advice supply an affective toolkit through which parents make sense of their feelings and experiences of family within a framework that feels natural. Equally, it is possible to argue that emotional attachments in families do not simply happen but are instead constructed – actively made and remade through what the sociologist David Morgan (1996) has termed 'family practices' (that is, the everyday habits, routines, and taken-for-granted rules of conduct through which family life is made up).

In arguing that emotional attachments between parents and children are taught and learned, the chapter adopts what is often, if somewhat loosely, referred to as a 'social constructionist' perspective. Social constructionism contains various strands of thought that do not always sit comfortably alongside one another. As such, it is better thought of as a tendency than a coherent body of ideas. However, despite these differences, it is possible to identify a number of common orientations that help distinguish social constructionism from other approaches. In particular, social constructionist arguments emphasise meaningful human activity or social practice in the making of social worlds. As sociologists Peter Berger and Thomas Luckmann wrote in what was one of the first major statements of a social constructionist position, 'despite the objectivity that marks the social world in human experience, it does not thereby acquire an ontological status apart from the human activity that produced it' (Berger and Luckmann, 1966, p. 78). What they meant by this was that, even though the social world often appears to us to be simply 'there' – a bit like a mountain range or chemical element – it is, in reality, in a state of constant construction. It is made and remade as we go about our daily lives, by the meanings and practices that constitute these. Following on from this, social constructionists often argue that phenomena that we tend to assume to be given in nature will often, on closer inspection, turn out to be aspects of the social world – that is to say, the outcome of meaningful human activity. For this reason, social constructionists often advocate placing even our most basic concepts and understandings 'under erasure' – suspending our belief in them in order to investigate how a particular phenomenon comes into being.

As such, a social constructionist approach is liable to address parent – child attachments in ways rather different from those adopted in more conventional accounts. It might be expected, for example, that a chapter on parent – child attachment would begin with the work of John Bowlby (1966), the influential founder of 'attachment theory'. Bowlby argued that 'love in infancy and childhood is as important for mental health as are vitamins and proteins for physical health' (Bowlby, 1966, p. 158) and went on to suggest that such love promotes a 'secure psychological attachment', one that provides the basis for both a positive sense of self in later life and for the ability to build healthy relationships with others (see the Introduction to this volume).

However, while many of Bowlby's arguments are extremely powerful, from a social constructionist point of view, they risk starting in the wrong place. For example, one of the most influential of Bowlby's ideas – or, at least, the popularised version of these that came to inform post-war childcare policy and practice – was the notion that, in order to avoid problems associated with maternal deprivation, mothers should be constantly available to their children. This implied that mothers could not go out to work or leave their children in daycare without putting at risk their children's emotional and psychological development (see Riley, 1983, pp. 92–108). This chapter will argue that the assumption implicit in this position – that it is women who are necessarily responsible for childcare and thus their children's psychological and emotional well-being – is one that is fundamentally flawed. Close emotional attachments between mothers and their children can be said to arise, not from biology, but from the way in which parenting is socially organised. Bowlbyism failed to see this because, rather than investigating how emotional attachments are actively made and maintained, it simply assumed that a mother's role in loving her children is given by nature. It is, then, in the questioning of such taken-for-granted assumptions that the utility of the social constructionist perspective is to be found. Rather than assuming the existence or naturalness of a given phenomenon (in this instance, mother-child love as something ordained by nature), social constructionism obliges us to ask *how* it came about in the first place. In refocusing the lens of enquiry in this manner, social constructionist approaches 'defamiliarise' the world around us, 'making strange' what we might otherwise fail to see (Bennett and Watson, 2002).

In order to pursue these issues, the remainder of this chapter is organised into five sections. Section 2 picks up the argument that we began to explore in the preceding paragraph, outlining the feminist social constructionist claim that close emotional attachments between women and children result from the social organisation of parenting rather than any straightforward biological imperative. Sections 3 and 4 then move on to explore some of the social resources that can be said to shape and inform the social practices of parenting. Section 3 focuses, in particular, on the widespread assumption that gender-specific forms of parenting arise out of biological differences between men and women – for example, that women's responsibility for childcare is somehow rooted in something that can be labelled 'biological femaleness'. In contrast, Section 4 explores the 'feeling rules' that can be said to shape parents' intimate contact with their children – for example, in relation to what is considered appropriate or inappropriate about bathing or kissing. The penultimate section then goes on to investigate the ways in which parents can be said to use emotional attachments with their children to actively 'make up' the family (Hacking, 1986) and asks whether increasing investments in children compensate in some way for the decreasing stability of adult intimate relationships. Finally, in the conclusion, the chapter reflects on what parent – child attachments might have to tell us about two of the core sociological 'concerns' identified in the Introduction to this book: mediation and the relationship between the individual and the social.

1.1 Teaching aims

This chapter explores social constructionist readings of parent – child relationships, aiming to develop a critical understanding of these and, therefore, of family attachments. In particular, it suggests that:

■ Emotional attachments between parents and children – particularly those between mothers and children – arise from the social organisation of parenting practices and not nature.

- Parents draw upon social resources in making, maintaining and policing the boundaries of relationships with children.

- Families are actively 'made up' through social practices, and that emotional attachments with children in part compensate for the increasing fragility of adult relationships.

- Social constructionist arguments can be used to advance our understanding of 'mediation' and 'the individual and the social'.

2 Parenting as a social practice: feminist accounts

Andrea: *I think the love that you have for your children is ... it's just different. It's a protecting ... it's a love that you'd do anything. You'd stand in the way of any danger or anything and it's your responsibility to protect them, take care of them. Also the fact that they're part of you ... it's unconditional no matter what ... I just think from the moment that you have your child it's a natural thing that you want to protect them and that you love them ... I think people can divorce or split up or whatever and move on. I would find that really hard to do that with my children. I don't think I could close the door on my relationship with a child.*

Like Ann (whose quotation opened this chapter), this mother, Andrea, talks about motherhood in terms of a lifelong emotional investment or 'unconditional' love, one that develops as the foetus gestates in the mother's womb and remains throughout childhood as she cares for and nurtures her offspring. For Andrea, this love clearly feels profoundly natural. However, as the introduction to this chapter suggested, from a social constructionist perspective, even our most visceral feelings can be misleading. For social constructionists, emotions, such as love, are neither intuitive nor individual, even though they may be experienced as such. Instead they are structured through culturally available social repertoires of feelings (Jackson, 1993; Redman, 2002). This does not mean the feelings themselves are 'wrong'. Andrea obviously loves her children very much and we can imagine that they are an important and fulfilling part of her life. What might be misleading in this instance is, then, not the feelings that Andrea has for her children but her assumption about where these feelings come from. While Andrea clearly understands her feelings about her children as reflecting the natural order of things, it is possible to argue that, in reality, they reflect the way in which parenting is currently organised in Western social formations. In short, it is possible to argue that emotional attachments between mothers and children do not arise from nature but from the social worlds in which we live.

Some forty years ago, feminist commentators began to question the widespread assumption that women and children were destined – that is, ordained by nature – to be together. Having enjoyed unprecedented access to paid work during the Second World War, the post-war years saw the reassertion of traditional ideas in which women's 'natural' role was assumed to be that of mother and homemaker. From the mid 1960s onwards, this vision of mothering came under increasing criticism from so-called 'second wave' feminists (the first wave of feminism referring to women's struggles for the vote in the late nineteenth and early twentieth centuries). In particular, feminists drew attention to the inequalities and restrictions such notions imposed on women's lives. Women's lack of educational and career opportunities; inequalities in domestic labour; and the sheer drudgery and hard work of raising small children, often in isolation from other people, all came under scrutiny (see, for example, Gavron, 1968; Oakley, 1974).

Perhaps unsurprisingly, some strands within this feminist critique were overtly opposed to the idea that mothering was or could be a positive experience for women. For instance, in a memorably pungent passage, one capturing the polemical sentiments of much radical feminist thought of the time, the North American feminist Shulamith Firestone wrote: '*Pregnancy is barbaric*. ... Pregnancy is the temporary deformation of the body of the individual for the sake of the species. Moreover, childbirth *hurts*. And it isn't good for you. ... Childbirth is at best necessary and tolerable. It is not fun. Like shitting a pumpkin' (Firestone, 1979 [1970], pp.188–9; emphases in original).

However, most feminist commentary was not so determinedly anti-mothering, instead recognising that mother-child relationships are experienced by many women as individually fulfilling and emotionally rewarding. Rather than criticising motherhood per se, this strand of feminist scholarship sought to separate the experience from the institution (Rich, 1984), suggesting that it is the *social organisation* of mothering which is problematic and not maternity itself (Comer, 1974; Richardson, 1993). This argument has been extended in more recent feminist scholarship which has drawn attention to the diversity that exists in the social organisation of mothering. Research on, for example, lone mothers (Silva, 1996), lesbian parents (Gabb, 2005), and the lives of those outside dominant white culture (Collins, 1994) has highlighted the fact that mothering is not a single, unitary phenomenon. Rather, social practices of mothering vary across cultures, time and social groups.

From a social constructionist perspective, the most interesting feature of these feminist arguments is this latter emphasis on mothering as a socially organised practice. Once motherhood is conceived of in these terms – something one *does* rather than someone one *is* – it becomes possible to argue that mothering can be done by a range of people including men and those biologically unrelated to the child concerned. This perhaps suggests that there is nothing peculiarly special about the mother-child relationship. While babies and children may well need a continuity of love and care, nature does not itself privilege the biological mother as the provider of this. There is nothing in nature, social constructionists argue, that demands that once a child has left a woman's body, that same woman must care for it. As the existence of wet nurses attests, for certain classes even breastfeeding has historically been carried out by women other than babies' mothers. Feminist philosopher Sara Ruddick evokes something of this argument's potential when she writes that, one day, there could be 'mothers of both sexes who live out transformed maternal thought in communities that share parental care' (Ruddick, 1983, p. 227).

Figure 1.1
Shared parenting. One day could there be mothers of both sexes?

Where does this leave Andrea's feelings about her children? As we have said, nothing in feminist arguments questions the authenticity of Andrea's feelings. What they do suggest, however, is that her access to these feelings is dependent on the way in which parenting is socially organised. In other words, Andrea has an intense emotional attachment to her children not because nature prescribes that mothers feel this way but because the social organisation of parenting means that it is she who does the close emotional work with her children. We can see this more clearly if we compare the following extracts: the first from a research diary kept by Helen, the mother of a nine-year-old son, Ben; the second from an interview with a father, Henry:

Helen: *Took Ben to the doctor's first thing. He was very nervous. I held his hand the whole time we were in the waiting room. The rest of the day we spend together with lots of loves and cuddles in the chair and on [the] sofa later watching TV ... Ben slept with me in [the] spare bed ... Lots of cuddles. Ben woke me up by putting his arm round me and stroking my face.*

Compare this with Henry's comments on his relationship with his son and daughter, Harry and Kelly:

Henry: *[W]hen he was younger [we used to play fight but] as time went by Harriet [Henry's wife] seemed to get close to Harry and I seemed to draw back ... I felt as if I wasn't giving enough affection. I still liked to cuddle him and the same thing's happened to Kelly a bit. Harriet seems to get close to Kelly and Harry and I still struggle to get close ... I think it's more of a physical thing.*

What is perhaps most striking about these extracts is the close, practical character of the emotional care and support Helen provides her son and the relative distance of Henry's relationship with his children. This distance has not come about because Henry is a 'bad' father nor, it is possible to argue, is it the case that fathers are 'naturally' distant while mothers are 'naturally' close to their children. Indeed, Henry seems to regret his lack of closeness. Instead, Henry's distance from his children seems to derive from the way in which parenting is socially organised. Unlike his wife Harriet, Henry is simply not as involved in the intensive, ongoing work of providing his children with emotional nurturance and support.

Men's frequently expressed sense of loss about their lack of intimacy with their children (see, for instance, Lupton and Barclay, 1997) graphically illustrates the ways in which emotional attachments in families do not just happen, as if by some natural process, but are instead actively made and maintained via the social meanings and practices of parenting – most specifically, those practices of intimacy and care that women carry out as mothers. As Helen's comments suggest, these involve real emotional benefits for the women concerned, not least in the pleasure and sense of personal fulfilment they bring. However, we should probably be wary of romanticising the social practices of mothering. The care and support of children is, at the best of times, physically demanding and emotionally draining. Despite this, the social organisation of parenting, not only in Europe and North America but also in many other societies, is such that a disproportionate burden falls on women. This is apparent in the following extract:

Helen: *I get up at 7 and I get my shower and I get myself done by 7.30 and then go wake the boys and start getting them rousted ... Martin [husband] gets up well he doesn't he wakes up, he lays in bed, he'll watch his news, he'll get up at 7.40, he'll have a shower, he'll see to himself, he comes down at 8 o'clock grabs a slice of toast and he's out by 8.05 ... whereas I've been up like a whirlwind ... but you see if he had to do that he just wouldn't be able to do it, he just couldn't cope because he hasn't got the patience.*

Helen's experience is not atypical. Many women have to structure their daily routine around the lives of their children and family, often while also engaged in other activities. Helen justifies why she does the morning childcare duties on her own by saying that her husband 'just couldn't cope'. She does not elaborate on why he 'hasn't got the patience'; it is something which is part of family life, something that she has to work around. Her acceptance of the disproportionate childcare duties simply becomes part and parcel of her role as mother.

There is, of course, some evidence that, in Northern Europe, contemporary patterns of parenting are beginning to shift away from this conventional division of household labour (Brannen and Nilsen, 2006). Indeed, the anxiety of fathers, like Henry, to build and sustain parent – child attachments, albeit in distinctive (gendered) forms, may well reflect this. Whether or not this is so, the shift does not yet seem to have progressed very far and there remain relatively few men involved in the more mundane aspects of childcare (Sullivan, 2000). However, the fact that these shifts are happening at all is interesting because they serve to demonstrate the social construction of gendered parental categories, roles and responsibilities. If the organisation of parenting can change, then the parental roles and the everyday family attachments built out of these cannot be said to be given in nature but must instead be rethought as the outcome of social meanings and practices. Indeed, as fathering and mothering become more interchangeable, the sex/ gender distinctions that have been invoked to shore up traditional patterns of parenting may well lose credence. Social changes demonstrate the temporariness of affective patterns and evince their fabrication in the social practices that make up family life. In this way the *social process of parent – child attachment* becomes evident.

3   Biological sex and the 'naturalisation' of parenting practices

As we saw in the preceding section, social constructionists argue that the intimate attachments characteristic of mother – child relationships are not, as is often assumed, simply given in nature but are instead the outcome of social meanings and practices of nurturance and care. If this is so, why do many women experience their feelings for their children as profoundly natural? Why, for instance, should Andrea, the mother whose comments began the last section, appear passionately to believe in the naturalness of mother – child 'unconditional' love?

One of the most persuasive answers to this question focuses on the assumption, widely held in contemporary Western social formations, that biological sex is the foundation of, and determines a diverse range of, social phenomena. For instance, biological maleness is widely assumed to have, as one of its inherent characteristics, a propensity towards aggression. In this light, various social phenomena, such as war and violent crime, are often explained in terms of this inherent propensity. Men, we are told, are 'naturally aggressive' and therefore predisposed to violence whether at home, in the form of domestic violence, or outside the home, in the form of warfare. In the same way, biological femaleness is widely assumed to have as one of its inherent properties a propensity towards the reproduction and raising of children. So strong is this assumption that women who do not have children sometimes experience themselves as, in some sense, 'incomplete' in their gender.

From a social constructionist perspective there are a number of problems with this biologically determinist argument. The first of these, already identified in the previous section, concerns the way in which women's ability to bear children is conflated with the demand that they also raise them. As previously discussed, social constructionists point out that, once a child has left its mother's body, there is no reason in nature why she should be primarily responsible for its care. Such care can be (and frequently is) provided by other people, both women and men. The second problem social constructionists raise in relation to the biologically determinist argument is more subtle. Is it actually the case, they ask, that biological sex exists? Might it be a social category, something we impose *on* nature rather than something inherent *within* it? Something *learned* rather than something that we *are*?

One of the most prominent exponents of the argument that biological sex is the outcome rather than the foundation of gendered social practices (like those of parenting) is the North American feminist philosopher and social theorist Judith Butler. In her celebrated book

Gender Trouble, Butler sketched the main contours of this position. For instance, she wrote:

> Gender ought not to be conceived merely as the cultural inscription of meaning on a pregiven sex ...; gender must also designate the very apparatus of production whereby the sexes themselves are established. As a result, gender is not to culture as sex is to nature; gender is also the discursive/cultural means by which 'sexed nature' or 'a natural sex' is produced and established as 'prediscursive,' prior to culture, a politically neutral surface *on which* culture acts. ... one way the internal stability and binary frame for sex is effectively secured is by casting the duality of sex in a prediscursive domain.
>
> (Butler, 1990, p. 7)

Similarly, she argued, 'Gender is the repeated stylization of the body, a set of repeated acts within a highly rigid regulatory frame that congeal over time to produce the appearance of substance, of a natural sort of being' (Butler, 1990, p. 33). As these quotations indicate, Butler's main point is that our bodies become culturally intelligible as 'sexed' through social practices. In the context of families and parent – child relationships, her argument suggests that repeated gendered social acts (such as those of parenting) help constitute female/male sexed differences as 'prediscursive' (that is, pre-social). As such, gendered parental practices can be said, in Butler's (1993) words, to **materialise** bodies as either female or male: to 'attribute' or 'write' maleness and femaleness in to them. As this implies, rather than having a natural basis, our sexed bodies can be said to be created in part through everyday gendered practices.

On first hearing, this argument can sound surprising, perhaps even bizarre. There are, after all, rather obvious bodily differences between what we take to be males and females, one of which is the ability to bear children. Social constructionists certainly do not dispute such differences. Their point is rather whether it makes sense, on the basis of these, to identify two distinct sexes: male and female. For instance, they draw attention to the fact that, while all cultures seem to distinguish to some degree between maleness and femaleness, not all divide human beings into two separate biological groups. As the historian, Thomas Laqueur (1990) has demonstrated, it was only towards the end of the eighteenth century that a two-sex model began to take hold in European societies. Before this, people tended to conceive of themselves as belonging to a single sex in which femaleness was understood as an inferior version of a more fundamental maleness. Equally, the feminist anthropologist, Henrietta Moore (1994) has documented numerous cultures in which maleness and femaleness have been seen (to varying degrees) as either present in everyone or as two possibilities among

Figure 1.2
Playing house. Social practices 'materialise' bodies as female or male

a wider number of variations. For example, she writes that, although the Hua people of Papua New Guinea differentiate between male and female, they view maleness and femaleness as residing in particular bodily substances, not just external features such as the genitalia. Since these substances are said to be transferable between individuals, the Hua 'insist that the gender of a person changes over their lifetime as their body takes on more of the substances and fluids transferred by the other sex' (Moore, 1994, p. 90). In other words, for the Hua, maleness and femaleness are not discrete categories but are, or come to be, present in everyone. Seen in this light, the two-sex model appears less a *feature* of nature than a social category through which people in the social formations of the West attempt to *describe* or make sense of nature and the variations present within it (for example, the ability to bear children).

What does this argument have to tell us about the social practices of parenting? It suggests that things we often assume to be inherent features of biological sex (women's 'natural' propensity to be emotionally close to their children; men's 'natural' propensity to be more distant) do not, in fact, arise from biological femaleness or maleness but are instead means by which biological sex is *imputed* to human bodies. This is because, within Western social formations, motherhood and fatherhood are assumed to 'speak' or be synonymous with biological sex. To be a mother is, automatically, to be female; to be a father is, by necessity, to be male. If, however, maleness and femaleness are social categories, descriptions *of* rather than properties inherent *within* human bodies, then we can say that, as a woman enacts the social practices of mothering, so she has biological sex attributed to her (that is, she is 'made up' as female). Similarly, we can say that, as a man enacts the social practices of fatherhood, so he has biological sex attributed to him (which is to say, he is 'made up' as male). From a social constructionist perspective, the individuals involved then routinely *mistake* these attributions for features of nature. In other words, they assume that biological sex precedes social practices and, in so doing, they imagine that biological sex somehow determines the social practice itself. This is to say, they experience the social practice (mothering or fathering) as the natural *outcome* of a pre-existing biological sex.

From this point of view, we can begin to read Andrea's comments about the naturalness of her feelings for her children in a rather different light. Andrea, it is possible to argue, imagines that her feelings are natural because she experiences being a mother as somehow grounded in biological sex, as if raising children is an inherent property of this. From a social constructionist perspective, however, Andrea is 'made up' as female as she enacts the social practices of loving and caring for her children; she experiences the apparent 'fact' of her femaleness as the origin and cause of the fact that she loves her children.

This distinction is of more than purely sociological interest since it has real consequences for how men and women live their lives. As we saw in the previous section, many people – both men and women – take it for granted that women are somehow 'naturally' fitted for the work of childcare and that men are 'naturally' ill-fitted to this role (hence Helen's comments that her husband 'just couldn't cope' with getting the children up and ready for the day). The assumption that parenting practices are determined by biological sex is thus directly implicated in the unequal division of household labour identified in the previous section and in the relative exclusion of fathers from the closeness and intimacy that mothers often enjoy with their children.

4   Affective boundaries: setting the parameters of appropriate behaviour

As the previous section demonstrated, it is possible to argue that parents' belief in the 'naturalness' of their feelings for their children has its roots in the notions of biological sex current in contemporary Western social formations. However, the two-sex model is not the only social resource informing the practices out of which parent – child attachments are constructed. For instance, the ways in which parents define and negotiate the boundaries of appropriate/inappropriate affective behaviour with their children can also be said to draw on socially available values, beliefs and conventions.

To investigate this possibility, the *Behind Closed Doors* study asked mothers and fathers to comment on a picture, taken from a parenting handbook, of a man (presumably the father) sharing a bath with a child. Their responses to this picture highlight how and where affective boundaries are constructed around demonstrations of parent – child attachment. Claire's answer was typical:

Claire: *[T]here's nothing wrong with dads and their children [sharing a bath], I know it's difficult nowadays because of all the changes in, in erm, well the sensationalism around the child abuse and things like that. It's quite sad because it's preventing so much contact between children and their parents. Yes you've got to be a lot more vigilant and a lot more professional when, when you are working with children, but in a family situation no, there's absolutely no reason why not. It's part of growing up and understanding development and things like that as well.*

Interviewer: *What if this, this man was an uncle or a family friend?*

Claire: *Probably keep the intimacy within the family rather than a family friend or an uncle ... I don't think [that] would be appropriate.*

What Claire's answer shows us is that, for her, parent – child attachment can and even should involve bodily contact and intimacy but that the innocence of such activities should not be taken for granted. While concerns over child welfare are nothing new, it is true to say that, at least in Northern Europe and North America, they began to appear in a particularly intensified form in the last decade of the twentieth century. Stories of male predation and child abuse became part of most families' affective agenda, encouraging parents to be on their guard and vigilant to protect their children from harm. This has increasingly caused intergenerational exchanges to be measured in terms of what constitutes 'normal' behaviour. For Claire, like many other parents, the degree of affection and intimacy that is permitted is determined through measuring the normality of the activity against the closeness of the relationship between male adult and child. What is appropriate intimacy between 'close' family members (and we should probably remember that how closeness is measured will vary between social groups) is inappropriate once extended beyond immediate family – 'just in case'. Claire expresses certainty that she knows what is and is not acceptable without feeling any need to justify herself. She simply 'knows' right from wrong and appears to presume the interviewer will share her views. Claire's confidence on this point

Figure 1.3
Bath time. Social rules of behaviour shape family practices

suggests the existence of a social consensus around the boundaries of intergenerational embodied behaviour. Parents' individual management of the boundaries of affect and sexuality can thus be thought of as drawing on shared social understandings that tend to be couched in terms of risk and morality and focused around the needs of children.

One of the most obvious sources feeding this consensus is to be found in the plethora of material offering advice on how to be a 'good parent' (although it should be acknowledged that what constitutes 'good' varies depending on the source consulted). This parenting advice is mediated knowledge. For example, at the time of writing, parents in the UK were bombarded with, *inter alia*, 'professional knowledge' mediated through handbooks and magazines; 'expert' advice delivered in the form of reality television programmes such as *Super Nanny* (Channel 4) and *Little Angels* (BBC3); and websites, such as ThinkBaby, providing instant access to ideas and guidance, some of which are commercially sponsored (ThinkBaby, 2007; see also BBC, 2007).

Such guidance is often clear about bodily boundaries and typically advocates the need to protect children from 'risk', especially sexual predation. However, somewhat paradoxically, it cannot be said to provide hard and fast rules on how to navigate everyday embodied boundaries in parent – child relationships. Instead, parents have to rely on what *feels* right, experienced as intuition or common sense, while all the time taking on board media hyperbole around instances of child abuse and adult – child victimisation. This inevitably results in a degree

Figure 1.4

Parenting magazines. Mediations of 'good parenting' advice abound

of uncertainty around physical contact between children and adults, especially men. Comforting, rough-and-tumble play and routine embraces are risky practices, as they are *at risk* of being misunderstood. As Morgan writes, 'Parents, especially fathers, may express confusion as to what is now expected of them in the context of widespread concerns about the sexual abuse of children' (Morgan, 1996, p. 124). Nowhere is this more complex than when children push at the boundaries of appropriate/inappropriate behaviour, forcing parents to deal with 'embarrassing' and/or 'risky' situations, as is illustrated by Ann:

Ann: *[S]nogging [passionately kissing] is a funny thing with children because, I think that sometimes they watch it on television and they want to try and snog you know like. But I don't remember snogging when I was seven. I, I mean Ollie [son] is a very affectionate child, this family is affectionate and we often we give him lots of kisses and cuddles but erm I probably, I probably would discourage him from snogging, you know ... I think it's, I think it's perfectly fine to kiss your child on the mouth, like a kiss on the cheek, on the head, you know. Erm but I don't think children are there, my own personal view is children ... are not there to be snogged, you know ... I think it's perfectly reasonable to say no, we don't do snogs. We do kisses but we don't do snogs, and that. And maybe they see, children see their mum and dad having a kiss and they'll they copy or they see it on the television. They want to try and do that but for me it would be reasonable to say no we don't do that ... Because we teach them, don't we that, that there are rules of affection, I suppose.*

If we look closely at what Ann says, we can see the way in which she draws on mediated cultural resources and shared understanding of what is right and wrong but, at the same time, uses these to construct and consolidate a position of her own. She lays out her own understanding of the differences between different types of kissing and what is correct parent – child affection. She segments the child's body into areas that are acceptable and those that are prohibited for parents to kiss. She mentions how television and adult interactions can influence children's affective behaviour and that it is the parents' role to educate children – that is to say, to show them what is age-appropriate and culturally acceptable behaviour. She substantiates her position by making reference to her own childhood. Finally, in the concluding sentence she presupposes consensus between herself and the interviewer (and, by implication, a wider public) by adopting a shared viewpoint – 'we teach them, don't we ...'.

One way we can understand this process – parents' dependence on pre-existing and shared social resources and the various ways in which these are deployed by different individuals as they attempt to negotiate and make sense of a given situation – is through what the North American sociologist Arlie Hochschild (2003) has called **feeling rules**. Hochschild suggests that, faced with an emotional experience, we are aware both of our feelings (perceived as intuitive) and the cultural 'guideposts' that shape these feelings. Referring to various anthropological studies, Hochschild demonstrates how feelings take on *meaning* only in relation to a specific time and place in the world. Conformity with these cultural rules is achieved through spoken and unspoken sanctions and social conventions which instruct us and/or reassure us about how to feel, letting us know that our feelings are legitimate – hence, for instance, Ann's assuredness that she speaks for us all; she knows *the* rules. It is this taken-for-granted knowledge that feeling rules are 'natural', common sense, an agreed 'normal' way of being and behaving which makes them different from other rules.

As Hochschild outlines in Reading 1.1 below, feeling rules are distinct from other types of rules because emotions are typically understood as '*a precursor to action*' (emphasis in original), a motivating factor rather than a response and as such they are 'resistant to formal codification' (Hochschild, 2003, p. 99). As you read the extract you may want to reflect on the ways in which, despite this absence of formal codification, people's emotions are nevertheless rule-bound.

Reading 1.1   Arlie Russell Hochschild, 'The commercialization of intimate life'

The capacity to feel

An image on the movie screen, a passage in a book, the look in an eye can move us deeply. But what in us is moved? How does culture help do the moving? How do sociologists understand the role culture plays? ...

...

Feeling rules

We feel. We try to feel. We want to try to feel. The social guidelines that direct how we want to try to feel may be describable as a set of socially shared, albeit often latent (not thought about unless probed at), rules. In what way, we may ask, are these rules themselves known and how are they developed?

To begin with, let us consider several common forms of evidence for feeling rules. In common parlance, we often talk about our feelings or those of others as if rights and duties applied directly to them. For example, we speak of 'having the right' to feel angry at someone ... We know feeling rules, too, from how others react to what they infer from our emotive display. Someone may say to us, 'You *shouldn't* feel so guilty: it wasn't your fault,' ... At other times, a person may, in addition, chide, tease, cajole, scold, shun – in a word, sanction – us for 'misfeeling.' Such sanctions are a clue to the rules they are meant to enforce.

Rights and duties set out the proprieties as to the *extent* (one can feel 'too' angry or 'not angry enough'), the *direction* (one can feel sad when one should feel happy), and the *duration* of a feeling, given the situation against which it is set. These rights and duties of feeling are a clue to the depth of social convention, to one final reach of social control.

There is a distinction, in theory at least, between a feeling rule as it is known by our sense of what we can *expect* to feel in a given situation and a rule as it is known by our sense of what we *should* feel in that situation. ...

...

Whether the convention calls for trying joyfully to possess, or trying casually not to, the individual compares and measures experience against an expectation that is often idealized. It is left for motivation ('what I want to feel') to mediate between feeling rule ('what I should feel') and emotion work ('what I try to feel'). Much of the time we live with a certain dissonance between 'ought' and 'want', and between 'want' and 'try to.' But the attempts to reduce emotive dissonance are our periodic clues to rules of feeling.

A feeling rule shares some formal properties with other sorts of rules, such as rules of etiquette, rules of bodily comportment, and those of social interaction in general. A feeling rule is like these other kinds of rules in the following ways: It delineates a zone within which one has permission to be free of worry, guilt, or shame with regard to the situated feeling. A feeling rule sets down a metaphoric floor, walls, and ceiling, there being room for motion and play within boundaries. Like other rules, feeling rules can be obeyed halfheartedly or boldly broken, the latter at varying costs. A feeling rule can be in varying proportions external or internal. Feeling rules differ curiously from other types of rules in that they do not apply to action but to what is *often taken as a precursor to action*. Therefore they tend to be latent and resistant to formal codification.

Feeling rules reflect patterns of social membership. Some rules may be nearly universal, such as the rule that one should not enjoy killing or witnessing the killing of a human being. Other rules are unique to particular social groups and can be used to distinguish among them as alternate governments or colonizers of individual internal events.

Framing rules and feeling rules: issues of ideology

Rules for managing feeling are implicit in any ideological stance: they are the 'bottom side' of ideology. ... we can think of ideology as an interpretive framework that can be described in terms of framing rules and feeling rules. By 'framing rules' I refer to the rules according to which we ascribe definitions or meanings to situations. ...

...

As some ideologies gain acceptance and others dwindle, contending sets of feeling rules rise and fall. ... What we call the changing climate of opinion partly involves a changed framing of the same sorts of events. For example, each of two mothers may feel guilty about leaving her small child at daycare while working all day. One mother, a feminist, may feel that she should not feel as guilty as she does. The second, a traditionalist, may feel that she should feel more guilty than she does.

Part of what we refer to as the psychological effects of 'rapid social change,' or unrest, is a change in the relation of feeling rule to feeling and a lack of clarity about what the rule actually is, owing to conflicts and contradictions between contending rules and between rules and feelings.

Reading source

Hochschild, 2003, pp. 75, 97–100

Hochschild demonstrates how 'feeling rules' are constructed and maintained but she reminds us that particular shared feelings (for example, the assumption of parents' love for their children) do not yield predictable sets of action. As she writes, a feeling rule 'sets down a metaphoric floor, walls, and ceiling' but, within this, there is 'room for motion and play within boundaries' (Hochschild, 2003, p. 98). One reason for this is that our feelings are comprehended and mediated through our individual circumstances and life histories. However, they are also understood through social categories, including race, gender and age, that apply differently to different people. In consequence, we do not all share the same values. For example, not all parents will share Ann's opinions on 'snogging'. As this suggests, there may be many *legitimate* responses – 'sets' of feeling – which simultaneously remain within the 'rules' but which may significantly differ one from another. From this perspective, there is not a single correct template for parent – child attachment but varying interpretations and experiences, all of which must operate within the normative rules that define morally acceptable codes of conduct, but which allow for the particularities of individual, sociocultural circumstance.

We can view this process in action in the following extract. Jeff (a single-parent father) and his friend Lydia clearly hold a markedly different opinion about parent – child 'snogging' from the one expressed by Ann earlier in this section, yet all three parents believe theirs is the normal viewpoint:

Lydia: *I'd find it funny, I'd just laugh it off.*

Jeff: *I'd just say to her 'Oh that was nice' [laughter]. Not in* that *sense of the word.*

Lydia: *No but they might take it as that.*

Jeff: *Well let them take it as that.*

Lydia: *The best way is just to laugh it off. It depends what the situation were and in that situation it's just like a cuddle ... I mean if it was a total different situation and she had horrible parents and they were like abusing her or whatever, do you know, then that could be took totally different. That could be a sign that she's letting people know but in that situation it's just innocent and I'd laugh it off if I was the parent.*

In their attempt to reach a mutually agreed position, Jeff and Lydia clarify what they individually think. Jeff explains what he means by 'nice', making sure that we understand him (that is, nice means 'pleasant', not 'sexually enjoyable'). Lydia (as did Ann) explicitly positions her opinion and course of action as distinct from (potentially abusive) others. All three parents normalise their own individual position by claiming to know how to behave and the social rules that dictate how children *should* demonstrate affection.

Although Jeff's and Lydia's answers differ from Ann's, they demonstrate once again how culturally constituted rules shape parents' affective conduct – how attachments between parents and children are constructed out of and in relation to pre-existing social resources. However, the differences in the three responses underline the fact that, while feeling rules may set the boundaries within which parenting practices occur, they do not, in any straightforward sense, determine them.

5   The significance of children

Helen: *I think it's just developing that bond isn't it? It's that connection between those people. I suppose it's like the umbilical cord but it's like an emotional umbilical cord that you know is always there between you and no matter what happens, you grow up and you get your own lives but that connection is always going to be there and that closeness between you.*

In the last two sections, we have been exploring how parents draw on naturalising social meanings or discourses in order to understand and substantiate parent – child attachment. In this light, it is not surprising that, in the above quotation, Helen uses the metaphor of the umbilical cord to signify the naturalness and lifelong attachment between parents and children. However, it is possible to read Helen's comments as doing something over and above this. Helen seems to have invested strongly in the notion that children provide the physical – emotional glue that binds the separate individuals of a family together. What might be going on here?

One possible answer to this question can be found in the work of the German sociologists, Ulrich Beck and Elisabeth Beck-Gernsheim (1995). As we shall explore in more detail later in this section, they argue that children, in some sense, counteract the *fragility* of contemporary adult relationships. In order to investigate this point, in what follows we return to Ann, one of the mothers quoted earlier in the chapter.

At the time of the study Ann and her husband, Tom, were in their late thirties and their son, Ollie, was two years old. Both parents were in full-time employment, working in the field of child welfare. They were white, relatively affluent and lived in a large house in the leafy suburbs of a northern city in the UK. Observation of their everyday family life suggested Ollie was situated at the centre of Ann's and Tom's world. Virtually all conversations were directed at him with both parents constantly attending to his physical and emotional needs. Ann and Tom were receptive to any situation in which they could teach Ollie through play and their total commitment to his successful upbringing was very clear. They typically referred to each other as mummy and daddy and, on the few occasions where they spoke directly to one another, it was nearly always in connection with Ollie and his needs. These observations illustrate the intensity of their *family attachments*. With this in mind, we can look at further data from Ann's research diaries and interviews and consider how she and Tom constructed their family through their child.

Ann: *I reached out and took hold of Ollie's small hand. Ollie then held out his other hand and said 'daddy'. Tom reached across and held Ollie's other hand. Ollie smiled I said to Tom, 'How sweet is Ollie, he sees us [as] a family the three of us'.*

Discussing this entry in her diary, Ann reiterated the role of her child in creating family:

Ann: *I didn't know that children would do that, it would [be] like, he would, cos he was like 'mummy, mummy, mummy' or 'daddy, daddy', sort of you are two people. But the fact that he, he puts one arm out for Tom and one out for me and he pulls us together and that unites us as a family … he connects us together.*

In this extract, Ann appears to characterise Ollie as both the emotional glue that coheres the family relationship and the means by which they are socially recognisable as family. Ann, Tom and Ollie amount to something more than three separate individuals, they are a unit: a family. Moreover, the picture she conjures up does not simply ascribe social meaning to her son's actions. In describing her son's 'spontaneous' affective practices, Ann can be said to be 'making family', bringing it into existence. Needless to say, Ann does not create this story of family attachment out of nothing. Her description draws on the cultural repertoire of 'the family' that is available to her. Nevertheless, it can be understood as an active making of the family as a social institution.

As is apparent in the following quotation, this active making of families is one that extends beyond the immediate household:

Figure 1.5
Forging connections.
Families are created
through children

Ann: *Ollie is such a cuddly child, like we left my mum's house the other*
         day and I said to Ollie, 'Go give granddad a kiss', and Ollie ran, it
         was the most hilarious run, he ran that fast he flew into the room
         and he threw his arms round my dad and gave him a kiss and my
         dad just said, 'Oh that was priceless'. You know and my dad's not,
         erm, my dad doesn't kiss and hug us, erm, he's not a touchy person.

In this quotation, Ann suggests that attachments between Ollie and
those whom he loves not only unite intergenerational family members,
forging emotional and physical attachments between parent – child and
grandparent – child, he also breaks down gendered boundaries between
father and adult daughter. As a child, Ollie is blissfully unaware of the
tendency of men, in this instance his granddad, to show restraint and/or
discomfort around physical adult – child contact. This leads Ann to
perceive him as an affective bridge. He breaks down the boundaries that
have separated father and adult daughter. The use of the term 'priceless'
in this quotation suggests that this emotional openness is beyond
anything that can be purchased; its value is personal and precious to all
of them.

As this indicates, Ann and many other parents perceive their sense of
being family as something that is achieved through their children.
Parent – child attachments, it would seem, are, in Butler's (1993) terms,
materialised through children's intuitive expression of their feelings.
However, the closeness and constancy of these family attachments has
been questioned in research on contemporary interpersonal

relationships. This research typically suggests that, because of changes in the patterns of intimate relationships, families can no longer be defined as insular units that contain these but should more accurately be characterised as part of expansive *networks of intimacy*, networks that support or even usurp the former emotional privilege afforded to 'the family' (Jamieson, 1998, p. 77). One implication of this is that it may no longer be so pertinent to examine the structural, familial parameters of attachments. Instead, it may be more relevant to focus on the *quality* of personal relationships and how these relational ties are maintained through different acts and practices of care and intimacy (Williams, 2004). These arguments draw on the notion of individualisation which emphasises relational diversity and emotional transience. From this perspective, families are seen as affective 'patchworks' that are pieced together through attachments that shift along an individual's life course. The 'post-familial family' (Beck-Gernsheim, 1998) is an umbrella that brings together these attachments but does not contain them; parent – child and couple relationships typically rework the boundaries of these volitional affinities.

These ideas are explored in the following reading from an article by Beck-Gernsheim. As you read the extract, you should ask yourself what Beck-Gernsheim means by the 'patchwork' or 'post-familial' family.

Reading 1.2   Elizabeth Beck-Gernsheim, 'On the way to a post-familial family: from a community of need to elective affinities'

Individualization is understood as a historical process that increasingly questions and tends to break up people's traditional rhythm of life – what sociologists call the normal biography. As a result, more people than ever before are being forced to piece together their own biographies and fit in the components they need as best they can. They find themselves bereft of unquestionable assumptions, beliefs or values and are nevertheless faced with the tangle of institutional controls and constraints which make up the fibre of modern life ... To put it bluntly, the normal life-history is giving way to the do-it-yourself life-history. ...

...

[Women] can no longer think of themselves just as an 'appendage' of the family, but must increasingly come forward as individuals with their own interests and rights, plans and choices. ... Whereas traditional sociology always conceived the family as a unit with homogeneous interests and positions in life, there is now a contrasting focus on gender difference. ... [M]en and women are becoming visible as separate individuals, each linked to the family through different expectations and interests, each experiencing different opportunities and burdens. In short, the contours of distinctively male and distinctively female lives are now becoming apparent within the family.

...

Many divorced people later remarry or cohabit with a new partner who was also married before and may also have children of their own. More and more children thus grow up with one non-biological parent. ... [They] move backwards and forwards between their different family worlds, between the 'everyday parent' who has custody and lives with a new partner, and the 'weekend parent' who does not have custody and may also have a new family. This may well lead to complex relationship structures that can be presented only in diagrams with many ramifications. ... One key characteristic, of course, is that it is not clear who actually belongs to the family. There is no longer a single definition – that has been lost somewhere in the rhythm of separations and new relationships. Instead, each member has their own definition of who belongs to the family; everyone lives out their own version of the patchwork family.

...

In this constellation it is no longer the traditional rules of ascription (descent and marriage) which determine the family bond. The key factor now is whether the social relations stemming from it persist after the divorce. Where these relations are broken or gradually fade, there is also an end to the ties of kinship. What could be seen emerging in other family constellations of modernity is here fully displayed: maintenance of the family link is no longer a matter of course but a freely chosen act. In the situation following a divorce, kinship is worked out anew in accordance with the laws of choice and personal inclination – it takes the form of 'elective affinities'. ...

...

Whereas, in preindustrial society, the family was mainly a community of need held together by an obligation of solidarity, the logic of individually designed lives has come increasingly to the fore in the contemporary world. The family is becoming more of an elective relationship, an association of individual persons, who each bring to it their own interests, experiences and plans, and who are each subjected to different controls, risks and constraints.

As the various examples from contemporary family life have shown, it is necessary to devote much more effort than in the past to the holding together of these different biographies. Whereas people could once fall back upon rules and rituals, the prospect now is of a staging of everyday life, an acrobatics of balancing and coordinating. The family bond thereby grows more fragile, and there is a greater danger of collapse if attempts to reach agreement are not successful. Since individualization also fosters a longing for the opposite world of intimacy, security and closeness (Beck and Beck-Gernsheim, 1995), most people will continue – at least for the foreseeable future – to live within a partnership or family. But such ties are not the same as before, in their scope or in their degree of obligation and permanence. Out of many different strivings, longings, efforts and mistakes, out of successful and often unsuccessful experiments, a wider spectrum of the private is taking shape. As people make choices, negotiating and deciding the everyday details of do-it-yourself relationships, a 'normal chaos' of love, suffering and diversity is growing and developing.

This does not mean that the traditional family is simply disappearing. But it is losing the monopoly it had for so long. Its quantitative significance is declining as new forms of living appear and spread – forms which (at least generally) aim not at living alone but at relationships of a different kind: for example, without a formal marriage or without children; single parenting, conjugal succession, or same-sex partnerships; part-time relationships and companionships lasting for some period in life; living between more than one home or between different towns. These in all their intermediary and secondary and floating forms represent the future of families, or what I call: the contours of the 'post-familial family'.

Reference

Beck, U. and Beck-Gernsheim, E. (1995) The Normal Chaos of Love, Cambridge, Polity Press.

Reading source

Beck-Gernsheim, 1998, pp. 56–7, 59, 65, 66, 67–8

In this reading, Beck-Gernsheim argues that 'the family' has lost its 'natural' status as a fixed feature of Western society, held together through mutual needs and ties of obligation. In an earlier article written with Beck, Beck-Gernsheim extended this point to suggest that, as kinship ties have shifted, children have taken on a greater symbolic significance in the making of family relationships. Situating children at the centre of the affective equation, these authors suggest that, in response to the fragility of contemporary adult relationships, children have become the source of emotional security and lasting attachment in many parents' lives. They point to the compensatory role of children in the cultural context of serial adult-sexual relationships, suggesting that parents' emotional and financial investment in their children is a strategic response to this (Beck and Beck-Gernsheim, 1995). In an age of risk and uncertainty, Beck-Gernsheim argues, it is children who have become the reliable source of love, with parents privileging children's 'needs', sometimes to the detriment of adult – adult relationships (Beck-Gernsheim, 1998). Moreover, as Beck and Beck-Gernsheim suggest (1995, p. 72), it is 'only logical that men and women are developing strategies to protect themselves and reduce the risks of becoming emotionally exhausted' from their eternal quest to find 'true (adult-sexual) love'. This is to say, investment in a child represents a proactive emotional response to the failings of serial relationships. The 'unconditional love' experienced in the parent – child relationship fills the long-term emotional needs that are largely unrealisable elsewhere. The child, they write,

> promises a tie which is more elemental, profound and durable than any other in this society. The more other relationships become interchangeable and revocable, the more a child can become the focus of new hopes – it is the ultimate guarantee of permanence, providing an anchor for one's life.
>
> (Beck and Beck-Gernsheim, 1995, p. 73)

Looking at how Ann describes her attachment to her child, this emotional investment is perhaps evident:

Ann: *Put Ollie to bed, gave me a big cuddle, sang a song, stroked his hair and kisses goodnight. Stood and watched Ollie slowly close his eyes, open them, close them, open and close, then finally, eyes getting heavier, fall asleep with his arms wrapped around his toy dog. Priceless ... Reached the end of the diary. Looking back the whole focus is about Ollie. I think this reflects the depth of my feelings and love for my son ... the love you feel is not describable in words. It's a feeling from within that makes you feel a deep sense of happiness, nothing in comparison touches the same part.*

These sentiments are undoubtedly heartfelt but what is noticeable about them is the way in which they position the relationship between Ann and Ollie as if it is outside the social. In her professional capacity, Ann would be well aware of the fragility of kin relationships. She would know that families are frequently made and remade across a child's life course, structured around changing adult-sexual relationships. With this in mind, it is perhaps not surprising that she seems to work so hard to separate her own family (and by implication her relationship) from the wider social context. It is arguably the means by which she conjures up a sense of permanence for both.

In seeking to represent the materiality of parent – child attachments as natural, heartfelt, 'deep' (possibly also unconscious) emotions that forge a permanent connection, parents can be said to be actively disavowing the social construction of family life. Tom and Ann, for instance, appear to use the intuitive actions of their child to instantiate ideas of family. Ollie is presented as the creator of family and, as such, their family is constructed as an affective grouping that is prior to the social, a unit that is held together by the child's *instinctive attachment* to both parents. In doing so they aim (albeit unwittingly) to conceal the socially constructed basis of these relationships and their own connections to wider social networks which position them as just one family among many others; a social context within which one in sixty-five children in the UK is affected by divorce by the age of sixteen. By utilising naturalising discourses, which displace the social as the context for parent – child relationships, parents like Tom and Ann can be said to be positioning their families outside the shifting patterns of social trends. If the relationships are forged intuitively, *through the child*, their naturalness is irrefutable. The family is, in this light, not a social unit; it is a group of individuals bound together through durable, elemental, *natural* attachments. In this way, it can be said that parents instrumentally construct attachments by strategically drawing on naturalising discourses of parent – child and family attachment to claim permanence for these relationships.

6   Conclusion

The introduction to this chapter indicated that, by way of a conclusion, it would reflect on what a social constructionist understanding of parent – child attachments might have to tell us about mediation and the relationship between the individual and the social, two of the major sociological 'concerns' that are threaded throughout the book as a whole. In fact, these concerns have been implicit in much of the preceding argument. As you have seen, one of the chapter's major contentions centres on the claim that, even though parents' feelings about their children are often experienced as 'natural' or 'intuitive', it is possible to argue that they draw on (or are *mediated* by) social practices and available social meanings. For instance, Sections 2 and 5 both suggest that the structure of families and the roles people adopt within them are not simply given in nature but are, instead, the outcome of social practices that are historically contingent and culturally specific. Families are, in this view, made and remade through everyday practices of intimacy and care, and the routines of domestic life. In this light we can say that social practices are the medium through which families are constituted.

Similarly, as Section 3 argued, in describing their feelings for their children as 'natural', mothers can be said to be drawing on available social meanings of biological sex, social meanings that construct biological sex as something that precedes and thereby determines the social. Biological sex may *feel* like something that is simply 'there', but, social constructionists argue, it is in reality a social construct, a category that people in the social formations of the contemporary West impose on nature rather than something inherent to it. In other words, the social construction of biological sex mediates mothers' experience of their attachment to their children. Equally, as Section 4 argued, the 'intuitive' sense that parents often seem to have about what is appropriate conduct in relation to their children can, on closer inspection, be seen to draw on a repertoire of socially available 'feeling rules'. As such, these feeling rules can be said to mediate – to shape or filter – how parents think, feel and act in relation to their children.

Needless to say, to understand parent – child attachment as the outcome of social meanings and practices, rather than something giving rise to them, is also to challenge conventional understandings of the relationship between the individual and the social. Conventionally we might think of the individual as standing outside or prior to the social – something upon which the social builds. However, from a social constructionist perspective, this does not make sense. Social constructionists tend to argue that there is little of consequence that can be said to be 'on the side of the individual'. Rather, the attributes and capacities with which individuals are equipped are, they suggest, made by and in social meanings and practices. From this point of view, the capacities and attributes associated with, for example, motherhood (maternal love and care, say) do not reside 'inside' individual mothers but come into being – are materialised as Butler (1993) might put it – as women enact the practices of mothering. And what is true for mothers is true also for children, fathers, in fact people everywhere. The individual, from this point of view, exists only in relation to the social and the precise forms that individuality takes are those supplied by the social worlds in which the individual is located. As this chapter has sought to establish, this process can be demonstrated even in relation to phenomena, such as parent – child attachments, which we would usually consider to be given in nature or as otherwise lying outside or beyond social determination.

References

Beck, U. and Beck-Gernsheim, E. (1995) *The Normal Chaos of Love*, Cambridge, Polity Press.

Beck-Gernsheim, E. (1998) 'On the way to a post-familial family: from a community of need to elective affinities', *Theory, Culture & Society*, vol. 15, nos 3–4, pp. 53–70.

Bennett, T. and Watson, D. (eds) (2002) *Understanding Everyday Life*, Oxford, Blackwell/Milton Keynes, The Open University.

Berger, P. and T. Luckmann (1966) *The Social Construction of Reality: A Treatise in the Sociology of Knowledge*, Harmondsworth, Penguin.

Bowlby, J. (1966) *Maternal Care and Mental Health*, New York, NY, Schocken Books.

Brannen, J. and Nilsen, A. (2006) 'From fatherhood to fathering', *Sociology*, vol. 40, no. 2, pp. 335–52.

British Broadcasting Corporation (BBC) (2007) 'Parenting' [online], http://www.bbc.co.uk/parenting (Accessed 13 March 2007).

Butler, J. (1990) *Gender Trouble: Feminism and the Subversion of Identity*, London, Routledge.

Butler, J. (1993) *Bodies That Matter: On the Discursive Limits of Sex*, London, Routledge.

Collins, P.H. (1994) 'Shifting the center: race, class, and feminist theorising about motherhood' in Glenn, E.N., Chang, G. and. Forcey, L.R. (eds) *Mothering, Ideology, Experience and Agency*, New York, NY, Routledge.

Comer, L. (1974) *Wedlocked Women*, Leeds, Feminist Books.

Firestone, S. (1979 [1970]) *The Dialectic of Sex: The Case for Feminist Revolution*, London, Women's Press.

Gabb, J. (2001) 'Desirous subjects and parental identities: toward a radical theory on (lesbian) family sexuality', *Sexualities*, vol. 4, no. 3, pp. 333–52.

Gabb, J. (2005) 'Lesbian M/Otherhood: strategies of familial-linguistic management in lesbian parent families', *Sociology*, vol. 39, no. 4, pp. 585–603.

Gavron, H. (1968) *The Captive Wife*, Harmondsworth, Penguin.

Hacking, I. (1986) 'Making up people' in Heller, T.C., Sosna, M. and Wellbery, D.E. (eds) *Reconstructing Individualism: Autonomy, Individuality, and the Self in Western Thoughts*, Stanford, CA, Stanford University Press.

Hochschild, A.R. (2003) *The Commercialization of Intimate Life: Notes from Home and Work*, Berkeley, CA, University of California Press.

Jackson, S. (1993) 'Even sociologists fall in love: an exploration in the sociology of emotions', *Sociology*, vol. 27, no. 2, pp. 201–20.

Jamieson, L. (1998) *Intimacy: Personal Relationships in Modern Societies*, Cambridge, Polity Press.

Laqueur, T. (1990) *Making Sex: Body and Gender from the Greeks to Freud*, Cambridge, MA, Harvard University Press.

Lupton, D. and Barclay, L. (1997) *Constructing Fatherhood*, London, Sage.

Moore, H. (1994) 'Divided we stand: sex, gender and sexual difference', *Feminist Review*, vol. 47, Summer, pp. 78–95.

Morgan, D.H.J. (1996) *Family Connections: An Introduction to Family Studies*, Cambridge, Polity Press.

Oakley, A. (1974) *Housewife*, London, Allen Lane.

Redman, P. (2002) '"Love is in the air": romance and the everyday' in Bennett and Watson (eds) (2002).

Rich, A. (1984) *Of Woman Born: Motherhood as Experience and Institution*, London, Virago.

Richardson, D. (1993) *Women, Motherhood and Childrearing*, Basingstoke, Macmillan.

Riley, D. (1983) *War in the Nursery: Theories of the Child and Mother*, London, Virago.

Ruddick, S. (1983) 'Maternal thinking' in Treblicot, J. (ed.) *Mothering: Essays in Feminist Theory*, Totowa, NJ, Rowman and Allenheld.

Silva, E.B. (1996) *Good Enough Mothering? Feminist Perspectives on Lone Motherhood*, London, Routledge.

Sullivan, O. (2000) 'The division of domestic labour: twenty years of change', *Sociology*, vol. 34, no. 3, pp. 437–56.

ThinkBaby (2007) 'ThinkBaby' [online], http://www.thinkbaby.co.uk (Accessed 13 March 2007).

Williams, F. (2004) *Rethinking Families: Moral Tales of Parenting and Step-Parenting*, London, Calouste Gulbenkian Foundation.

Acknowledgement

Interview and diary extracts cited in this chapter come from an ESRC-funded project, *Behind Closed Doors: Researching Intimacy and Sexuality in Families* (RES-000-22-0854). Thanks to the research fellows, Dr Melissa Dearey and Dr Anne Fairbank, who collected empirical data for this project and to the families who welcomed the researchers into their homes and gave their accounts of family relationships.

Chapter 2
'I just wanted her out': attachment, the psycho-social and media texts

Peter Redman and Joanne Whitehouse-Hart

Contents

1 Introduction

While conducting research exploring people's emotional investments in media texts, a respondent told us about an incident arising from the third series of the UK television game show, *Big Brother* (2002). As anyone familiar with it will know, *Big Brother* involves a group of contestants who live together, cut off from the outside world but under almost constant scrutiny from an unseen viewing public and a largely invisible production crew. Week by week, viewers are encouraged to evict their least favourite contestant by contacting a telephone voting line.

During the episode in question, a contestant called Jonny offered one of his fellow housemates, Adele, a cup of coffee. Adele refused his offer politely enough but, as Jonny walked away, mouthed the words, 'F – – – off' to his retreating back. Enraged by what she took to be an egregious display of hypocrisy on Adele's part, our respondent felt impelled to vote for her eviction. Since her own phone was out of order, she was obliged to rush from the house to the local payphone. This, however, was in use. Becoming increasingly frustrated, our respondent found herself banging on the kiosk door. 'I just wanted to get her [Adele] out', she explained.

Figure 2.1

Jonny Regan and Adele Roberts: two of the contestants in the reality TV game show, *Big Brother 3*

Although not all of us will have banged on the doors of telephone kiosks, this woman's reaction is perhaps not too distant from the strong emotions that many of us feel in response to media texts. Of course, not all media texts trigger responses of this magnitude, but it is not uncommon for such things as books, films, and music to provoke emotional attachments. Examples of this kind illustrate the phenomenon we will be investigating in the course of this chapter: the process by which positive and negative emotional attachments, often of a passionate nature, are forged between people and media texts. In the previous chapter, you were introduced to a 'social constructionist' account of emotional attachment. As you will have seen, social constructionist accounts – such as Arlie Hochschild's (2003) notion of 'feeling rules' – tend to argue that feelings derive from social practices and the emotional codes or repertoires available in a given social context. In this chapter, you will be exploring a rather different approach to emotional attachment, one informed by psychoanalysis. From a psychoanalytic point of view, feelings speak of and give access to an 'inner world', one of which we are often only partially aware or which remains profoundly unconscious. As Nancy Chodorow (who is both a practising sociologist and psychoanalyst) writes:

> Psychoanalysis is first and foremost a theory about the creation of personal meaning in the clinical encounter [i.e. in analysis itself]. This encounter illuminates the power of feelings, the ways that powerful unconscious inner realities and processes shape, enliven, distort, and give meaning and depth to our experience. Psychoanalysis tells us why we feel deeply about certain things, certain experiences, and certain people and why these powerful feelings are part of a meaningful life.
>
> (Chodorow, 1999, pp. 1–2)

As this suggests, whereas a social constructionist account is likely to focus on the contingent social practices and 'rules' through which emotion work is 'done', an argument informed by psychoanalysis will inevitably pay far greater attention to the ways in which processes of emotional attachment and detachment can be said to be shaped and animated by an unconscious inner world, something that, although not divorced from the social world, cannot be reduced to it.

These arguments will be developed in some detail in Sections 3 and 4 of the chapter. In the former, you will be introduced to relevant psychoanalytic ideas, in particular the notion of 'transference', a process which is central to a psychoanalytically informed understanding of our relationship to media texts and other cultural objects. In Section 4, these ideas are then applied to a short piece of illustrative material: an exploration of our own experience of watching the game show *Big Brother*. However, before moving on to explore these arguments, the chapter will first outline how processes of attachment to media texts have been more conventionally understood in media studies. To this end, Section 2 will explore what are often referred to as the 'effects' and 'active-audience' approaches, both of which have tended to eschew the notion that unconscious processes are involved in the attachments forged between people and media texts. The final section of the chapter draws together the preceding argument and explores what it might have to tell us about a 'psycho-social' approach to the active audience (that is, one informed by an analysis of what is social in the unconscious and unconscious in the social). In so doing it also highlights two of the 'sociological concerns' identified in the Introduction to this book: mediation and the relationship between the individual and the social.

1.1 Teaching aims

The aims of this chapter are to:

- Explore how attachments between people and media texts are forged.

- Introduce and evaluate competing explanations of this, specifically: the 'effects' and 'active-audience' approaches; and one informed by psychoanalysis.

- Explore the implications of psychoanalysis for a 'psycho-social' understanding of mediation and the relationship between the individual and the social.

2   Audience research: 'effects' versus the 'active audience'

As the previous section indicated, the main aim of this chapter is to explore a psychoanalytic or 'psycho-social' approach to the processes by which attachments are forged between people and media texts. However, before embarking on this task, we need first to situate the argument within more conventional accounts. Writing in the introduction to an edited collection on media audiences, Marie Gillespie (2005a) suggests that commentaries on the relationship between media texts and their audiences often draw on one of two traditions, emphasising either the *effect* that media texts have on their audiences or the *uses* to which media texts are put by them:

> [The first tradition] concentrates on *media effects* and asks 'what do the media do to audiences?' The media are seen as powerful and audiences as passive and vulnerable, prone to manipulation and easily influenced. The other focuses on *media uses* and interpretations and asks 'what do audiences do with media?' 'How do audiences use and make sense of media?' This approach tends to see audiences as more active and selective, creative and powerful.
>
> (Gillespie, 2005a, p. 2; emphases in original)

Perhaps the most famous example of an 'effects' approach can be found in the celebrated 'Bobo doll' experiment conducted by the social psychologist Albert Bandura (Bandura et al., 1961). Under experimental conditions (i.e. conditions seeking to minimise influences other than those being tested in the experiment), Bandura and his colleagues sought to show whether or not viewing screen violence (a large Bobo doll being hit by an adult) influenced children's actions (see Figure 2.2). Sonia Livingstone, in a useful overview of the 'effects' literature, explains what happened:

> Social learning theory proposes that people learn to imitate what they see only if they see the behaviour being rewarded and not if they see it being punished. And this is what happened in Bandura's experiments. Children who saw a film of rewarded aggression were more likely to imitate the aggressive behaviour afterwards in the playroom than were children who saw punished aggression in the film or those who saw no aggression at all.
>
> (Livingstone, 2005, p. 25)

Figure 2.2
Bandura's Bobo doll experiment: children who had viewed a film in which aggression was rewarded were more likely to behave aggressively themselves

For media effects theorists, these and other results like them indicate that media texts can and do cause people to act in particular ways. For example, Livingstone quotes a committee of psychologists who, in a parliamentary briefing to the UK Government, asserted, 'screen violence can desensitise viewers, raise aggression levels, reduce empathy for victims and enhance the role of violence in conflict resolution' (Parliamentary Office of Science and Technology, 1993; quoted in Livingstone, 2005, p. 23).

However, while few commentators deny that the media have an impact on us (why, for example, would people often be scared in horror movies if this were not so?), many are sceptical of the strong version of the 'effects' argument: that media texts *determine* or control our feelings, actions or thoughts. For example, even apparently persuasive scientific evidence, like that available from Bandura's Bobo doll experiment, is open to question. As Livingstone (2005, pp. 25–26) explains, the effect Bandura and his colleagues observed (that watching violence on screen led to violent behaviour in young children) has proved difficult to replicate in real-world settings, such as nurseries. This indicates that any effect the media may have is heavily dependent on or mediated by the *context* in which the text in question is consumed. Media texts, it would seem, do not simply reproduce us in their image – cause us to think or behave in particular ways – rather, we *actively interpret* or make sense of them using the resources available to us in the social worlds in which we are located.

We can explore this point via a well-known art historical example. At the Paris Salon of 1765, the artist Jean-Baptiste Greuze won public acclaim for his painting *Une jeune fille, qui pleure son oiseau mort* (see Figure 2.3).

Figure 2.3

Une jeune fille, qui pleure son oiseau mort, 1765, by Jean-Baptiste Greuze (1725–1805)

'A girl crying – for her dead bird'

Contemporary writers, including the great Enlightenment encyclopedist, Denis Diderot, reviewed the painting in ecstatic terms, yet, as the art historian Emma Barker (2005, p.1) has commented, 'Greuze criticism today takes it as axiomatic that viewers no longer respond to his work in the way that his original audience did'. She writes:

> [F]or anyone seeking to demonstrate what the problem is, *Une jeune fille, qui pleure son oiseau mort* provides a convenient case in point. It is

an example of the so-called 'Greuze girl', a type of picture that has above all served to damn the artist's name. ... The fundamental accusation is that Greuze's paintings are contrived and artificial, that he at once manipulates and panders to his audience by gratifying a self-indulgent (and hence incipiently perverse) desire for emotional arousal. Even Anita Brookner, whose important 1972 monograph marked the beginning of a continuing reappraisal of the artist, betrays a certain embarrassment about his procedures. She comments, for example, that the pictures Greuze submitted to the Salon of 1765 'can be seen as an exploitation of every point on which he had ever won public approbation – uplifting, sentimental and decently pornographic'.

(Barker, 2005, pp. 1–2)

How is it that a sophisticated eighteenth-century audience could be profoundly moved by *Une jeune fille, qui pleure son oiseau mort*, yet to modern eyes the painting appears 'contrived and artificial', even 'sentimental and decently pornographic' (the dead bird being an allegory of lost virginity)? The answer, as Barker goes on to explain, lies in the fact that modern viewers lack the cultural competence to experience the painting as it was experienced by contemporaries. To eighteenth-century eyes, the painting was an exquisite example of what Barker identifies as 'sentiment'. For Greuze and his contemporaries, she explains, sentiment referred both to the innate emotional capacity to be 'touched and moved, above all by the sight of a fellow human being in distress' and also to the proper organisation of this capacity in 'a stable and unified state of mind', one embodying 'conviction, conscience and consciousness' (Barker, 2005, p. 9). Thus, what to us may look merely sentimental, trite or perhaps (because of its implied eroticisation of adolescent girls) 'incipiently perverse', appeared to contemporary eyes as something far more serious and moving, even morally improving.

The implication of this argument is, of course, that the painting itself does not programme a particular effect in its viewer. Instead, this effect is mediated by the viewer's active interpretation of the painting, an interpretation that is necessarily dependent on the interpretative competencies, aesthetic dispositions and classificatory practices available to the viewer in the social world in which he or she is located (Bourdieu, 1984). Thus, even if, like Anita Brookner, we can today admire Greuze's formal qualities as an artist, we cannot re-enter the precise social world in which *Une jeune fille, qui pleure son oiseau mort* was originally painted and received. We cannot see it through the eyes of Diderot and his contemporaries.

This **'active-audience' approach** – one focusing on what audiences *do* with media texts or the uses to which they put them – has, in its various, sometimes competing guises, dominated the analysis of media texts over the last thirty years. From the point of view of this chapter, one of the most interesting aspects of this diverse body of work has been its emphasis on what Lawrence Grossberg (1992, p. 52) calls people's constant struggle to make texts mean in ways 'that connect to their own lives, experiences, needs and desires'. As this suggests, for proponents of the active-audience approach, the process of consuming media texts – even those sometimes derided as trite or trashy – is assumed to be intensely meaningful. This is illustrated in Gillespie's (2005b) discussion of the work of US-based Egyptian anthropologist Lila Abu-Lughod. In one study, Abu-Lughod (2002) describes a respondent, Amira, who was a passionate viewer of Egyptian television melodramas. Strikingly, Amira told her own life story using the conventions of these melodramas. As Abu-Lughod writes:

> Like the television dramas, the themes of [Amira's] story are money, with the villain trying to cheat her out of hers, and the secret, with the truth about her sinister husband discovered too late. The melodramatic heroine, innocent and good, is wronged and victimized. Seeking a better life ... she leaves the village and home to find herself overworked, underpaid, and hungry in a house where the food is locked up. Seeking love, companionship, or respectability ... she finds herself betrayed.
>
> (Abu-Lughod, 2002, p. 124)

Abu-Lughod (2002, p. 123) even suspected that Amira's emotionally wrought personal style ('She was often embroiled in conflicts and arguments – with her sister, her employers and her neighbours') was also borrowed from the same source. Why should Amira be passionately attached to melodramatic television serials and choose to tell about (and perhaps live) her own life in their terms? Abu-Lughod's answer is that television melodramas helped Amira make sense of the highly individualised circumstances in which she found herself. Amira was, as Abu-Lughod (2002, p. 122–4) explains, a migrant, separated from her family, living alone and reliant on her own labour for survival. Although she longed to locate herself within the conventions of traditional Egyptian society – in particular, those of family – this option was simply not available to her. The conventions of melodrama furnished her with an alternative. In casting herself as a vulnerable individual beset by troubles, Amira was able to make some kind of sense of her life.

As these examples imply, the 'active-audiences' tradition in cultural and media studies provides us with a powerful account of the processes by which emotional attachments between people and media texts are forged. From this perspective, people invest in particular media texts because these help make sense of and negotiate the contradictions of their lives. However, despite the strengths of such explanations, from a psychoanalytic point of view they are at best one-dimensional. This is because they have only a limited sense of those dimensions of experience that are not conscious and rational: what Chodorow, quoted earlier in the chapter, calls the 'powerful unconscious inner realities and processes [that] shape, enliven, distort, and give meaning and depth to our experience' (Chodorow, 1999, p. 2). With this in mind, the next two sections of the chapter begin to explore psychoanalytic arguments more systematically. What, they ask, do we mean when we talk about 'unconscious inner realities' and how might these shape and infuse our consumption of media texts?

3   Understanding the unconscious

Have you ever felt that an argument you are having with a close friend or a sexual partner is not really to do with the other person – that it seems to have come from somewhere else? Have you perhaps felt as though you were driven compulsively to say and do certain things and to relate in destructive ways? Have you ever felt as if you are mixed up with another person so that it is difficult to tell sometimes where you end and the other person begins? Have you ever wondered about the force of an attraction to someone, sexual or otherwise? Or have you ever wondered what happens when intense love suddenly gives way to disillusionment? Have you ever heard yourself complaining bitterly about another person and then realised that you were talking about an aspect of yourself?

(Thomas, 1996, p. 158)

This passage, written by a psychoanalytic psychotherapist, is quoted at the opening of an introduction to psychoanalytic theory by the cultural and media researcher, Jessica Evans. Commenting on the quotation, Evans writes that it draws our attention to the 'existence of the unconscious ... and the way it presses upon, and interferes with, everyday life, interactions and relations' (The Open University, 2000, p. 13). As Evans goes on to argue, it is this – the existence of a realm of unconscious life and its consequences for the rest of experience – that is the 'basic idea' of psychoanalysis, one that stands at its very heart, both as a body of ideas and a clinical practice.

On first hearing, the observation that the mind is capable of unconscious as well as conscious activity may sound rather commonplace. We know, for example, that we routinely remember telephone numbers without having constantly to hold them in our conscious thoughts. They are, for the majority of the time, 'unconscious' and we recall them to consciousness only when we need to use them. However, when psychoanalysis talks of unconscious activity it is referring to something rather different from, and more significant than, examples of this kind. For psychoanalysis, these are instances of 'pre-conscious' mental phenomena: things that are available to consciousness but not attended to in a given moment. In contrast, from a psychoanalytic point of view, **the unconscious** refers to processes – thoughts, feelings, images, impulses, emotional textures, the experience of bodily sensations – that are not easily available to conscious thought and that, frequently, remain profoundly inaccessible and opaque. For psychoanalysis, the unconscious is an 'inner' psychic reality or world which, in the words of psychoanalyst Susan Isaacs, has 'a continuous living reality of its own, with its own dynamic laws and characteristics, different from those of the external world' (Isaacs, 1952, p. 51; quoted in Dawson, 1994, p. 31). As this suggests, when psychoanalysis speaks of the unconscious, it is referring to a particular and irreducible dimension or register of the mind, one that is radically different from, but no less important than, those more familiar from conscious and pre-conscious thought.

With this in mind, it might be supposed that, as an 'inner reality' or 'system in its own right', the unconscious is divorced from external reality, a separate, hermetically sealed sphere. However, this is not the case. As Evans (quoted above) noted, the unconscious is said to 'press on and interfere with' our conscious experience and our relations with others. Thus, although its content may be unavailable (or not easily available) to conscious reflection, psychoanalysts argue that the effects of unconscious activity can be traced in conscious thought and observed in human interactions. Indeed, as you will see later in the chapter, many psychoanalysts go much further than this to argue that 'external' and 'internal' worlds are irretrievably intertwined, such that the social is always present in the unconscious and the unconscious in the social. In the rest of Section 3, we will begin to explore the implications of these arguments for a more sociological understanding of the processes by which attachments are forged between people and media texts. To this end, you will be reading part of Chapter 1 of Chodorow's (1999) influential study *The Power of Feelings*. As you will see, the extracts that make up the readings in the chapter are not directly concerned with the relationship between media texts and the unconscious. However, in foregrounding the ways in which unconscious activity can be said constantly to mediate our experience of people, objects and events in the external world, the extracts lay the foundation for a psychoanalytically informed version of an active-audience approach.

3.1 Transference, projection and introjection

You should now read the first extract from Chapter 1 of Chodorow's (1999) *The Power of Feelings*. Don't worry if, on first reading, it seems a little dense or if a number of the concepts it uses – for example, transference, projection, introjection and fantasy – are unfamiliar to you. We will discuss these concepts and the extract's main arguments after the reading.

Reading 2.1   Nancy J. Chodorow, 'The power of feelings: personal meaning in psychoanalysis, gender and culture'

Psychoanalysis is a theory about how we create personal meaning, our unconscious psychic reality, through what I am calling the power of feelings. 'Feelings' here encompass feeling-based stories or proto-stories – unconscious fantasies – that constitute our unconscious inner life and motivate our attempts to change that inner life to reduce anxiety and other uncomfortable or frightening affects or to put such uncomfortable affects outside the self. Several psychoanalytic terms, descriptions of emotionally laden psychodynamic processes that themselves overlap or can be translated one into the other, most clearly describe for us this creation of personal meaning. They include transference and, incorporated in it, projection and introjection, all of which express and create unconscious fantasy. The capacities that enable us to create personal meaning – capacities for transference, projection, introjection, and unconscious fantasy – are innate human capacities that develop and unfold virtually from birth, in a context of interaction with others. [...]

Transference is the hypothesis and demonstration that our inner world of psychic reality helps to create, shape, and give meaning to the intersubjective, social, and cultural worlds we inhabit. [...] Psychoanalytic investigation suggests that people are motivated or driven, in order to gain a sense of a meaningful life and manage threatening conscious and unconscious affects and beliefs, to create or interpret external experiences in ways that resonate with internal experiences, preoccupations, fantasies, and senses of self-other relationships. In transference, we personally endow, animate, and tint, emotionally and through fantasy, the cultural, linguistic, interpersonal, cognitive, and embodied world we experience. Stephen Mitchell likens transference to a prism: 'The patient's subjective world is organized like a prism whose facets refract and disperse entering illumination into customary and familiar wavelengths' (1993, 212). Christopher Bollas calls transference 'the private language of the self' (1987, 61):

Figure 2.4
Nancy Chodorow is a practising psychoanalyst and sociologist

'Our external world evokes unconscious elements of the self as object relation, and ... our experience of reality is therefore influenced by those unconscious associations elicited by environmental conditions' (1987, 48).

In a transference, we use experiences and feelings from the past to give partial meaning to the present as well as to shape the present, as we act and interpret present experience in light of this internal past. At the same time, it can also be said that through transference our current unconscious feelings and fantasies – contemporary psychic reality, whatever its temporal origins – give partial meaning to and shape conscious feeling and experience. [...]

Projection (sometimes called externalization) and introjection (sometimes called internalization), as these express unconscious fantasy, are the major modes of transference. In projection and projective identification, we put feelings, beliefs, or parts of our self into an other, whether another person with whom we are interacting, an internal object or part-object that has already been created through projective-introjective exchanges, or an idea, symbol, or any other meaning or entity. In introjection and introjective identification, aspects or functions of a person or object are taken into the self and come to constitute and differentiate an internal world [...] All projection and introjection express unconscious fantasy, an affect-laden image or account, often nonlinguistic, nonverbal, and simply sensed, of what the nature of the object is, what the object's intentions are, how the self can or should react or is liable to be affected by the object, what the effect of the self-object interchange might be on both, and so forth.

References

Bollas, C. (1987) The Shadow of the Object: Psychoanalysis of the Unthought Known, New York, NY, Columbia University Press.

Mitchell, S.A. (1993) Hope and Dread in Psychoanalysis, New York, NY, Basic Books.

Reading source

Chodorow, 1999, pp. 13–15

As you will probably have recognised, the central argument mobilised in this extract concerns **transference**. In classical psychoanalytic thought, this term was used to refer to the way in which psychoanalytic patients (analysands) 'transferred' feelings about significant figures from their childhood (typically, mothers and fathers) on to their analyst

(Freud, 1990 [1905]). Chodorow, however, uses the term in an expanded form, describing it as 'the hypothesis and demonstration that our inner world of psychic reality helps to create, shape, and give meaning to the intersubjective, social and cultural worlds we inhabit'. What does this mean? As Chodorow indicates, the suggestion here is that external reality – whether people, objects or events – is always, in part, experienced through or mediated by a 'screen' of unconscious activity or 'fantasy'. (It is probably worth stressing that such fantasy is understood to be unconscious and should not be confused with daydreaming or others forms of conscious thought – although the latter may well be tinged with the former.) Chodorow argues that, mediated by unconscious fantasy, our experience of external reality is given a particular shape, colour and emotional texture. In other words, it takes on the contours of our inner world. It is this shaping and colouring that Chodorow designates as transference.

Chodorow then goes on to argue that transference has two primary 'modes' – projection and introjection. As she explains, the first of these, **projection** (or its variant, projective identification), is a mechanism or capacity by which, in unconscious fantasy, we 'evacuate' parts of ourselves into external others or objects which are henceforth experienced as possessing the quality in fact belonging to us. It is as if we are unconsciously saying, 'This is not part of me, it is part of you'. (You may have noticed that Chodorow also says that we project aspects of ourselves into 'internal objects', a term that will be explained later in this section.)

Since, on first meeting, the notion of projection can sound somewhat strange, it is probably worth exploring via some concrete examples. In his classic text on the subject, the North American psychoanalyst, Thomas Ogden (1979, p. 358) argues that projection often involves an unconscious wish 'to rid oneself of a part of the self'. This occurs, he explains, either 'because that part threatens to destroy the self from within, or because one feels that the part is in danger of attack by other aspects of the self and must be safeguarded by being held inside a protective person' (Ogden, 1979, p. 358).

To illustrate the latter state (the unconscious fear that a 'good' part of the self is in danger from other, 'bad' parts and must, in consequence, be kept safe by projecting it into another person), Ogden cites the example of a young schizophrenic patient who, he writes, 'vehemently insisted that he … was only coming to his sessions because his parents and the therapist were forcing him to do so' (1979, p. 358). Ogden explains that, in reality,

> this 18-year-old could have resisted far more energetically than he did and had it well within his power to sabotage any treatment attempt.

However, it was important for him to maintain the fantasy that all of his wishes for treatment and for recovery were located in his parents and in the therapist so that these wishes would not be endangered by the parts of himself that he felt were powerfully destructive and intent on the annihilation of himself.

(Ogden, 1979, p. 358)

In other words, the young man in question was unconsciously projecting the part of himself that wanted to be helped into his parents and the therapist with the result that, consciously, he imagined it was they who were insisting on his need for treatment. As Ogden explains, this projection served to protect a part of him that was relatively healthy from other parts that were corrosive and undermining.

If this illustrates projection used as an unconscious mechanism to protect a 'good' part of the self, what of the second type of projection Ogden identifies: that motivated by the unconscious fear that a 'bad' part of the self will destroy the self from within? We can usefully illustrate this second type of projection via an example from another of Ogden's papers, 'The concept of internal object relations' (Ogden, 1983). In this, he cites the example of a twenty-year-old patient who was 'preoccupied with his anxiety concerning a particular male teacher whom he experienced as extremely intimidating' (p. 235). Ogden explains that the anxiety had its origins in a part of the young man that was identified with his 'bullying father'. In other words, there was a largely unconscious aspect of the young man's inner world that bullied and attacked other parts of this world. Ogden suggests that, to avoid the pain to which this gave rise, the young man unconsciously projected this bullying part of himself into the male teacher, who was henceforth consciously experienced as dangerous and likely to attack him.

As both of these examples demonstrate, projection involves the unconscious fantasy that part of the self belongs to another (whether a person or object). In contrast, the second psychic mechanism Chodorow identified in her discussion of transference – **introjection** (or its variant, introjective identification) – involves taking in to the self 'aspects or functions of a person or object' from the external world, which, in consequence, 'come to constitute and differentiate [our] internal world'. This last point is an important one. Previously we said that, via transference, the external world is mediated or processed – that is, shaped, coloured and given emotional texture – by unconscious fantasy. As you now know, this mediation is said to occur primarily through projection: the bringing of people and objects in the external world to subjective life by investing them with aspects of the self. The concept of introjection implies that the internal world of the unconscious is, in its turn, shaped, coloured and given texture – in fact, constituted and differentiated – by the taking in of 'aspects or functions' of the external world. The psychoanalyst Christopher Bollas captures something of this when he writes:

> I am inhabited ... by inner structures ... and in turn, I am also filled with the ghosts of others who have affected me. In psychoanalysis we term these 'internal objects,' ... *highly condensed psychic textures,* the trace of our encounters with the [external] object world. This suggests ... that as we encounter the object world we are substantially metamorphosed by the structure of objects; internally transformed by objects that leave their traces within us, whether it be the effect of a musical structure, a novel, or a person.
>
> (Bollas, 1993, p. 59; emphasis in original)

Introjection is, then, the process by which an unconscious inner world of internal objects is made and remade, in part, through the 'taking in' of aspects of people and objects found in the external world. Several things should be noted about this argument. First, internal objects are not said to be facsimiles of external people and objects but, as Bollas suggests, highly condensed psychic traces of our *experience* of them. As such, they are said to contain a 'self' component (what it felt like to be me in relation to the person or external object) and an 'other' component (what I imagined the person or external object felt like as it related to me) (see Ogden, 1983, pp. 234–6). Second, internal objects are not consciously known. As Bollas (1993, p. 59) goes on to write, they are 'inner presences that are the trace of our encounters, but not intelligible, or even clearly knowable: just intense ghosts who ... inhabit the human mind'. If we are aware of them at all it is more in terms of emotional texture and mood than anything consciously thought. Finally, it is these internal objects (or, more accurately, their 'self' and 'other' components) that are projected on to the external world.

3.2 Transference in everyday life

The examples of projection that we gave in the previous section were, as you saw, taken from the clinical context and were primarily defensive in character. This might be taken to suggest that transference is something that occurs only between patient and analyst and that projection is a product of mental ill-health, something the unconscious does as a way of avoiding more extreme forms of psychological pain. However, as you probably recognised from Chodorow's wider discussion in Reading 2.1, this is not her view. Instead, she sees transference, as it operates via unconscious fantasy, projection and introjection, as an integral part of everyday life and as something that, as well as being, at times, defensive, is also benign – indeed, life-affirming.

You should now read the second extract from Chapter 1 of *The Power of Feelings*, in which Chodorow takes up these arguments and expands them.

Reading 2.2   Nancy J. Chodorow, 'The power of feelings: personal meaning in psychoanalysis, gender, and culture'

[T]ransference is universal; what Freud discovered in the analytic encounter goes well beyond the specialized analytic relationship. Unconscious fantasies expressed in transference processes of projective and introjective identification are the way we give meaning to our lives and experiences in general. The capacity for transference [...] is thus one of the great abilities and defining capacities of the human mind. As Bird puts it, [...] transference is 'a universal mental function which may be the basis of all human relationships ... one of the mind's main agencies for giving birth to new ideas and new life to old ones' (1972, 267). We begin by investigating the analytic encounter – what goes on between analysand and analyst – but we rapidly realize that transferences are found *whenever* feelings, fantasies and emotional meaning are given to people and situations. Transference, projection, introjection, and fantasy are those continually active processes through which, in any immediate moment, we have the ability to bestow multiple emotional and cognitive meanings on perception or experience. These processes are an active and ongoing fact of life, and even within an analysis, they derive not only from early relations, situations, and people; they may also come from or be expressed in a person's current situation or in any important relationship or experience. [...]

Klein tells us that through projection, 'the picture of the external world ... is coloured by internal factors. By introjection this picture of the external world affects the internal one' (1963, 312). Robert Caper describes the radical implication of such a claim. From a psychoanalytic perspective, projection and introjection, expressing and mediating fantasy, act to enliven and make personally meaningful a world that is otherwise intrinsically meaningless: 'Klein believed that it is the balanced interplay of projection and introjection that produces, from the beginning of life, the dreamlike melding of internal and external reality that Freud discovered over and over to be the modus operandi of the unconscious. She could now also add that the same process is responsible for animating experience and making it psychologically meaningful. ... By investing the external world with emotions, positive and negative, projective identification animates it for the subject. This endowment enables one to find emotional meaning in the external world, permitting a subjective rather than a mechanical experience of it' (1988, 165, 232).

[...]

This perspective does not mean that the world is a projection without objective reality as we might observe its existence empirically; it means, rather, that our sense of the meaning of the world must come from within. Transference thus brings external objects to life *psychologically*, not in empirical fact. [...]

Two important and related claims are being made here. First, transference is ubiquitous, for it is the means by which we give personal psychological meaning to persons or experiences. Second, transference is psychologically necessary: without transference, our inner life, our relations to others, even our experiences of the physical world, would be empty and devitalized.

References

Bird, B. (1972) 'Notes on transference: universal phenomenon and hardest part of analysis', Journal of the American Psychoanalytic Association, vol. 20, pp. 267–301.

Caper, R. (1988) Immaterial Facts, Northvale, NJ, Jason Aronson.

Klein, M. (1963) 'On the sense of loneliness' in Klein, M. (1975) Envy and Gratitude and Other Works, New York, NY, Delta.

Reading source

Chodorow, 1999, pp. 21–3

Needless to say, this passage is not directly about media texts or their consumption. Nevertheless, together with Reading 2.1, it has important things to tell us about both. Previously we have suggested (paraphrasing Chodorow, 1999, p.2) that media texts are always 'shaped, enlivened, distorted and given meaning and depth' by unconscious meaning-making. We can now understand this claim in terms of transference, in particular the ways in which, in unconscious fantasy, media texts are brought to subjective life via the projection on to them of the self-other experiences that characterise internal object relations. With these arguments in mind, the next section begins to explore their implications for an 'active-audience' understanding of media texts. It does this via material from our own research on the UK version of the reality television game show, *Big Brother 3*, a series which aired in 2002.

4 Watching *Big Brother*

We originally became interested in transference and its role in people's responses to *Big Brother* as a result of our participation in a research group exploring a video archive from the show's third UK season. It was clear from the early days of the group's discussions that the show provoked strong feelings (just as it had done for the woman respondent cited at the start of this chapter). However, the possibility that transference processes might be heavily implicated in such feelings was brought home to us when we realised that one contestant – Jade Goody – was making Joanne Whitehouse-Hart feel distinctly uncomfortable.

Jade – who subsequently went on to build a successful career as a media celebrity – was, at the time she entered the *Big Brother* house, a twenty-year-old dental nurse, living with her mother in a council flat in a socially deprived area of South London. When the show was aired, Jade became the object of intense media interest. She had a tendency to fly off the handle or collapse in tears, displays of emotion that made her compulsive viewing. In addition, she was involved in a number of sexually-loaded incidents including an on-air encounter with a male housemate. However, Jade became most famous for being unschooled or 'thick'. She was unable to spell 'station', appeared not to know that Portuguese was a language, and, most famously of all, seemed to think that Cambridge was an area of London (it has to be said that it was never entirely clear how much of Jade's apparent 'thickness' was a genial if somewhat curious act).

Figure 2.5
Jade Goody, who became famous for being unschooled, went on to build a career as a media celebrity

Although Joanne's feelings about Jade were often tinged with sympathy (particularly during Jade's more vulnerable moments), they were predominantly ones of embarrassment. With her strong South London accent and 'street' mannerisms, Jade occupied an overt form of working-class femininity. Combined with her apparent lack of educational and cultural resources and her emotional outbursts, this seemed to stir up feelings that Joanne found difficult and painful. These feelings intensified in the context of the research group's discussions. The group was split between those who liked Jade, wanting to protect her, and those who disliked her, finding her 'snot and tears' and apparent attempts to gain sympathy irritating. Joanne was particularly nervous about responses of the latter kind. She was new to the group and perceived its other members as being more senior and – as someone who herself came from a working-class background – more middle class than she was. No matter how hard she tried to banish such thoughts from her mind, she kept thinking, 'Everyone thinks I am Jade'. Just as Jade had been ridiculed by the media, Joanne expected to be ridiculed by the group.

In the light of Chodorow's arguments, we can understand this as an instance of transference. From this perspective, we could say that Jade made Joanne nervous and embarrassed because she 'saw in her' something that, in unconscious fantasy, she had split off and disavowed in herself but that nevertheless continued to haunt her as a painful and only marginally thinkable 'presence'. If she expected the group to 'see this in her' and attack her for it, it was because she had somehow learned to experience this aspect of herself as 'bad' or worthless. As it turned out, the group did not see Joanne as 'Jade-like' and, as is the way with these things, the transference faded as Joanne settled into the group and became more comfortable with its other members. However, this had alerted us to the possibility that our own emotional responses to *Big Brother* might be an important resource in exploring the unconscious and its relationship both to media texts and to the social world.

The problem we faced was how to investigate this. Although psychoanalytic theory has been an important resource in film studies (see, for example, *Screen*, 1992), it has not been widely used in audience research. Indeed, the active-audience tradition emerged, in part, in reaction to these psychoanalytically informed studies of film which, in assuming that particular unconscious responses can be 'read off' from features internal to film itself, adopted what amounted to an 'effects' approach to film audiences. However, there was one obvious avenue for us to pursue. The prominent critical social psychologist, Valerie Walkerdine (1986, 1997) has conducted a number of media studies in which she reflects on her own biography and feelings, and the possible unconscious processes these may reveal. This practice draws on one common in clinical psychoanalysis in which the analyst attends to and reflects on the fleeting and often banal thoughts, feelings, memories and physical sensations she experiences while listening to the patient. These partial thoughts and half-formed feelings – often referred to as the analyst's 'reverie' – are said to register her 'countertransference': that which is stirred up in the analyst's unconscious by the patient's transference or, put another way, the analyst's transference in response to that of the patient. In attending to her own countertransference in this manner, the analyst hopes to gain insight into the patient's transference and thereby into the shape and climate of the latter's internal object relations (Ogden, 1994).

Needless to say, when watching *Big Brother*, we were not in the presence of the people portrayed on the screen. In consequence, our responses could not be said to have been stirred up by the transferences of the contestants on the show (i.e. they were not countertransferences). Instead, they were our own transferences on to *Big Brother* as a media text. Nevertheless, it seemed likely that, in attending to the fleeting thoughts, feelings and memories that occurred to us as we watched the show (in a manner similar to the analyst's reverie), we would gain useful insight into the processes by which *Big Brother* was given subjective meaning and brought emotionally to life. With this in mind, we decided to watch a week's worth of *Big Brother* programmes, recording after each, and in as uncensored a form as possible, the thoughts and feelings that had accompanied our viewing of it.

4.1 Investigating transference in *Big Brother*

The following is an extract from Peter Redman's research diary, written immediately after he had watched the first of the programmes we had selected for our task. As you will see, it focuses on a number of contestants, in particular, Sandy, a middle-aged Scot and former soldier; a young man named Spencer; and Lee, a muscular fitness instructor, who also happened to be black. You'll see that the notes also make passing reference to events in or features of the show. Although not directly relevant to our discussion, it may help you to know that: the 'task' mentioned in the opening paragraph was a competition, the winners of which were allocated to a 'rich' side of the house, while the losers were allocated to a 'poor' side; the wall mentioned in the third paragraph was the means by which the house was divided into rich and poor sections; Jonny (mentioned earlier in the chapter) and Kate were two other contestants on the show; and the chickens mentioned in the second paragraph were kept in the garden of the *Big Brother* house and were looked after by the contestants.

> I'm aware of being irritated by Sandy during the show. Certainly by the fact that he jumps in ahead of his turn in the weekly task and thereby secures his place on the winning side. Seems oddly childish or selfish – anyway, at odds with what I want him to be which is the mature, self-contained man in control, standing aloof from the foolish, shallow and over-eager throng. Am also troubled by his hatred for Jonny and Kate. This seems excessive. It's not just that he finds the antics of the others oafish or simpleminded: he hates them.

Although not unproblematically, Spencer does the self-contained man thing rather more systematically than Sandy although this isn't standing aloof from the crowd. There's a moment here where he's with Sandy talking about the chickens and I felt trying to get Sandy's attention or win his approval. Sandy was, though, slightly withheld – certainly not reciprocating fully. The cockerel that Spencer is talking to defecates provoking Spencer's disgust. I like him less in these moments: he's crude and laddish and makes me feel uncomfortable.

During the task and then when the housemates are sent off to pack up their stuff (prior to the wall going up) and then again when they come out of the bedrooms to find the wall in place, I'm mildly irritated by their over-eager chumminess. Reminds me of nervous boys talking too loudly and too brightly before exams at school and wanting to include you in their neediness. I noticed Lee in particular wanting to put his arms round people's shoulders. I would want to push him away. In fact, I find Lee very difficult: his size; his impregnable vacuity. Know I'd be slightly scared of him. Wouldn't know how to engage with him. Think he'd find me a waste of space.

Figure 2.6
Sandy Cumming, Spencer Smith and Lee Davey: three of the male contestants in the reality TV game show *Big Brother 3*

What are we to make of this extract? Perhaps the first thing to note is that at least some of the thoughts and feelings it contains are ones that Peter might usually be careful to censor, certainly keeping them hidden from other people and probably even from himself. As this implies, recording the flow of such thoughts and feelings makes visible a register of the mind that is seldom subject to conscious reflection, let alone accessible to others. In this vein, Thomas Ogden has written that:

> The analysis of [reverie] ... requires an examination of the way we talk to ourselves and what we talk to ourselves about in a private, relatively-undefended psychological state. In ... becoming self-conscious in this way, we are tampering with an essential inner sanctuary of privacy.
>
> (Ogden, 1994, p. 12)

As this suggests, for the individual concerned, the material generated by this practice is not always easy to contemplate and, particularly outside of a clinical context, may need to be handled with care. On the other hand, the analysis of such material promises admittance to a realm of experience that, for social researchers, would otherwise be largely opaque. Its shifting, fragmentary and sometimes elusive contents can, at the very least, be said to bear the traces of transference. As such, we would argue that, for the audience researcher, the attempt to capture and record transference in this manner is a productive, if sometimes uncomfortable, research practice.

So what does the method tell us in this particular instance? Although we believe the extract can be usefully read in psychoanalytic terms, it is first worth considering a more conventional sociological interpretation. This is because it has elements strongly suggestive of those practices of social categorisation by which, as the French sociologist Pierre Bourdieu (1984) has argued, members of one social group distinguish themselves from members of others. You may remember that, in Section 2 of this chapter, we argued that Greuze's paintings can appear sentimental to the twenty-first-century viewer because the interpretive competencies through which we read them are different from those available to an eighteenth-century audience. We can understand these interpretive competencies as forming part of what Bourdieu (1977) refers to as a person's 'habitus'; her or his taken-for-granted way of orientating to the world which includes such things as attitudes to, and the expression of, taste; modes of speech; and even ways of holding the body. Informally learned, largely in childhood, the contents of the habitus are said to become sedimented within us as particular 'dispositions', ways of relating to the world that do not determine our thoughts and actions in a given situation but which tell us – without our having to give the matter too much, if any, thought – how (at least in the terms of the habitus in question) something should be done and what constitutes good or bad behaviour or taste in that context (see also **Bennett, 2008**; Mauss, 1979 [1935]).

Seen in this light, we can read the extract's use of such phrases as 'oafish and simpleminded', 'crude and laddish' and 'impregnable vacuity' as indicative of the ways in which Peter was actively 'reading' the show in the terms of a middle-class, high cultural habitus. The disdain they seem to imply serves to distinguish Peter from the show's mainly young and working-class contestants and, by implication, from *Big Brother* as a form of popular entertainment. If the contestants are (in Peter's reading) 'simpleminded', then he, presumably, is not. If Spencer is sometimes 'crude and laddish', then Peter is presumably sophisticated and mature. If Lee is 'vacuous' then Peter has depth and complexity. In other words, these elements of the extract suggest that Peter was responding to or actively 'reading' *Big Brother* via the particular habitus he inhabits and which inhabits him. In the process he can be said to have been reproducing a particular social world (that of the white, middle-aged middle classes) and himself in its terms.

This more sociological reading of the extract is certainly productive and there can be little doubt that Peter's response to *Big Brother* was indeed shaped by the dispositions inculcated in him via the habitus to which he belongs. However, in our view, this tells us only part of the story. A closer reading of the extract suggests it is preoccupied with very *specific* aspects of Peter's habitus. In particular, it is not class per se that forms its central preoccupation but masculinity and age. For instance, Lee appears to be 'difficult' for Peter precisely because of his height and muscularity (and, we might imagine, because – within the terms of a white middle-class habitus – tall, muscular black men tend to be constructed as hyper-masculine). Similarly, the first paragraph's interest in the questionable nature of Sandy's maturity suggests that this is also a matter of some concern. These preoccupations with masculinity and age imply that Peter's response to the episode did not simply reproduce the forms of social categorisation characteristic of a middle-class habitus in general, but actively selected from these to make sense of the show in ways that were specific to Peter himself.

More significantly still, these preoccupations appear to have been accompanied by *anxiety*. Spencer's 'laddishness', for instance, made Peter feel 'uncomfortable', while Lee's size made him 'slightly scary'. Similarly, the contestants' response to the wall going up 'irritates' Peter, prompting a memory of 'nervous boys at school' waiting to enter the exam hall. In our view, the presence of anxiety in Peter's response to the episode suggests that his preoccupation with themes of age and masculinity was not wholly conscious or rational. In contrast to the arguments, such as Abu-Lughod's (2002), discussed in Section 2 of this chapter, Peter does not seem to have been 'negotiating' or attempting to make conscious sense of the material conditions of his existence. Rather, he seems to have been projecting on to *Big Brother* aspects of himself that he found troubling or difficult.

What might these aspects have been? A close reading of the extract suggests they were concerned with issues of vulnerability. For instance, when age appears in the extract it often seems to connote vulnerability and a demanding, sometimes selfish level of emotional need. Sandy's behaviour in the weekly task is, for example, described as both 'childish' and 'selfish', and this leads to an association in which Peter wants him to 'stand aloof' from a childishly 'over-eager throng'. The third paragraph returns to this theme more explicitly in the memory of boys waiting to enter the exam hall, whose nervous over-excitement is clearly identified as 'needy'. Similarly, the description of Spencer as trying to 'get Sandy's attention' not only positions him as younger than Sandy but as in some way vulnerable and requiring his 'approval'.

Of course, there may well be objective features of the episode in question which lent themselves to readings of this kind. However, we would argue that these features are not so strong as to demand interpretation in this manner. Instead, what seems to be happening is that, in these moments, Peter was projecting on to the contestants the 'self' component of an internal object relation (that part of the object relation in which we experience ourselves in the manner that the self was experienced as it related to the original external person or object). This 'self' component appears to have been one in which Peter experienced himself as variously, small, vulnerable, needy and demanding, potentially distressing feelings that, in the act of projecting them on to the *Big Brother* contestants, he was temporarily able to avoid in himself.

If we now examine those moments in the extract where masculinity is at issue, we will find they contain themes that parallel these feelings of vulnerability in interesting ways. For example, in the first paragraph, masculinity (specifically, the desire for Sandy to be the 'mature, self-contained man in control') seems to figure as the opposite of the demanding, child-like vulnerability identified above. It is perhaps not too far-fetched to read this as a moment in which, having (in unconscious fantasy) projected that part of himself that feels child-like and needy, Peter was able to experience himself as the 'mature, self-contained man in control', a position of relative psychological comfort and authority from which he could look down on the 'oafish and simpleminded' behaviour of the contestants.

However, this identification appears to be far more problematic later on in the extract. This is most obvious in the third paragraph where Peter imagines that he would be 'slightly scared' of Lee and that Lee would find him a 'waste of space'. Since there was little objective basis for this response (in fact, Lee was friendly and good-natured), we can plausibly understand it as an unconscious projection of an aspect of Peter's self identified with the 'other' component of an internal object relation (a part through which we experience ourselves in the terms that it is imagined the original external person or object experienced us). As you may remember, in Ogden's (1983) example, cited in Section 3.1, a twenty-year-old patient was described as projecting a bullying and threatening part of himself on to one of his teachers whom, in consequence, he found intimidating. In a similar vein, we can argue that Peter was projecting a threatening part of himself (one identified with the 'other' component of an object relation) on to Lee whom, in consequence, he also found intimidating. In the light of our previous discussion, we can at least tentatively suggest that this 'other' component is likely to have been one threatening to that part of Peter that felt small, vulnerable and needy. With this in mind, it is probably not surprising that Peter projected this threatening 'other' component on to Lee. To be small, vulnerable and needy is, of course, to lack a degree of masculine power. As a man who was large, muscular and black, we might imagine that Lee was, in Peter's unconscious fantasy, a particularly effective recipient for a projected aspect of himself that wanted to attack another aspect experienced as insufficiently masculine.

As with Joanne's reaction to Jade with which we began this discussion, this argument suggests that Peter's response to *Big Brother* was in part the result of transference (in fact, multiple transferences). Although he was perhaps not intensely caught up in the show (in the way that is sometimes the case when we watch, read or listen to media texts), Peter was undoubtedly emotionally engaged by it. As such, it would appear that, via the projection on to it of largely unconscious parts of himself, the show became subjectively meaningful to him – was animated and given emotional resonance.

This suggests the relevance of transference to an active-audience approach. Audiences, it can be argued, make meanings in part through unconscious fantasy and projection, actively selecting aspects of the habitus to process self-experience. Nonetheless, one objection that might be made to this argument is that, as a concept, transference is simply too static to be effectively integrated into an active-audience perspective. This is because internal object relations, often established in early infancy, might be said to 'pre-programme' transferences and, thereby, how media texts are read. In fact this is not so. As Chodorow (1999, p. 21) argued in Reading 2.2, transference is a 'continually active' process. It involves the active creation or bestowing of personal meaning in relation to the present and not simply the mechanical reproduction of a pre-existing meaning from the past. Elsewhere in the same chapter, Chodorow (1999, pp. 19–20) makes this point more explicitly, arguing that the transference that occurs in a given interaction cannot easily be predicted from either an individual's history of object relating or from the objective features of the interaction itself. Transferences, she tells us, can draw on unconscious experiences of self or other from the distant past; can involve material from the more recent past; and will respond to features of the present context. However, their exact content is not predetermined by any of these. Instead, transference involves the *active* selection by the unconscious of an object relation through which the present is experienced (Bollas, 1993, p. 42).

With this in mind, we can read Peter's response to *Big Brother* as an active making of unconscious meaning in the moment of his viewing. Of course, this does not mean that the forms of transference it involved came from nowhere. An individual's history of transference will often demonstrate elements of consistency and may even suggest that something about the individual's internal world is 'stuck' (hence the need for psychoanalytic treatment). Similarly, as the North American psychoanalyst Lynne Layton (2004) has argued, people sharing a habitus will often have overlapping projective fantasies about individuals and groups excluded from it. Indeed, the all too familiar tendency to attribute difficult or troubling characteristics to social groups other than one's own (for instance, the notion that particular groups of people are ignorant, lazy or in some way threatening) can be explained in precisely these terms (see also Chapter 5 in this volume). Yet, it is unlikely that, were he to watch the episode again, Peter would have exactly the same response to it. Equally, although they may echo Peter's transference to some degree, it is unlikely that, were other men to watch the episode, their response would simply replicate it. In short, while transference is not entirely random or without pattern, it is, in some fundamental sense, contingent and active.

Needless to say, in this particular instance, the forms of transference in play seem to have been ones that, although fairly mundane, were nevertheless defensive. In other words, the parts of Peter's self that were being projected were ones that were, in some sense, difficult or troubling. However, as was argued in Section 3.2, we need to remember that attachments to media texts, and the transferences through which they are mobilised, are often more benign than this and can sometimes be positively life-affirming. Bollas (1993, p. 29) has described these more positive moments as a form of 'lifting', instances when we are transported into intensely felt and deeply satisfying experiences of self. Whether positive or negative, however, transference can be seen as a significant means by which emotional attachments between people and media texts are forged.

5   Conclusion: towards a psycho-social version of the active-audience approach

In the course of this chapter we have sought to argue that, in order to understand the attachments – both positive and negative – that are forged between people and media texts, we need an account of the ways in which, via transference, such texts are rendered subjectively meaningful. An active-audience approach that is overly preoccupied with the conscious and rational dimensions of audiences' responses will, we have suggested, fail to capture this other register of experience, one that is arguably central to the often passionate nature of people's attachments. By way of concluding this argument, we want to clarify some of its main dimensions and, in the process, draw out its implications for what, in the introduction to the chapter, we called a 'psycho-social' account of the active audience. In so doing, we also aim to explore what these psycho-social arguments might have to tell us about mediation and the relationship between the individual and the social: two of the sociological 'concerns' identified in the Introduction to this book.

One objection that might be levelled against the argument the chapter has advanced is that, in focusing on the possible unconscious dimensions of attachment processes, it is addressing phenomena that are essentially internal and individual and not, therefore, properly sociological. It is certainly the case that the phenomena we have been investigating – transference, internal object relations, unconscious fantasy, projection and introjection – imply a depth of psychology and that to understand them we need forms of knowledge that lie beyond the formal boundaries of sociology and media studies. Nonetheless, as the chapter has, at various points, sought to argue, the boundaries between the unconscious and the social – and therefore between psychoanalysis and sociology – are rather more blurred than this might imply. Internal objects are a case in point.

As Section 3.1 argued, internal objects are constituted out of the individual's experience of people and objects in the social world. We are, as Bollas (1993, p. 59, quoted above) put this, 'internally transformed by objects that leave their traces within us'. As this implies, the unconscious is in part constituted by the social world. However, as Section 3.1 then went on to argue, via transference and projection, these internal objects in turn animate future social practices and interactions. This is to say that social practices and interactions – and the worlds they make and remake – are in part constituted out of material that is unconscious in nature. As 'external objects', aspects of these unconsciously infused social practices and interactions then become available for re-introjection, thereby reshaping our internal object relations. And so the process goes on, in what the cultural historian Graham Dawson (1994, p. 33) has called a 'spiralling circuit of psychic exchanges'. As this suggests, from this point of view, the notions of 'inside' and 'outside' are less useful than they might appear. The unconscious may be irreducible – may have its own level of determination and effects – but it is not separate from the social. Instead, it is always present in, indeed constitutive of, the social, just as the social is always present in, indeed constitutive of, the unconscious.

We would argue that understanding the social as being always present in the unconscious and the unconscious as being always present in the social indicates the possibility of a 'psycho-social' approach to the active audience, one attentive to both the psychic and the social dimensions of audience responses to media texts but able to grasp the mutually constitutive interactions between these. From this perspective, Peter's response to *Big Brother* can be said to have drawn on elements that were predominantly social (for example, forms of categorisation derived from his habitus), as well as elements that were predominantly unconscious (his internal object relations). Yet, via transference, these can be said to have been actively welded together in the moment of viewing to form what Bollas (1993, p. 18) calls an 'intermediate space', 'the place where subject meets thing ... a compromise formation between the subject's state of mind and the thing's character'. In this intermediate space, a social practice (watching a television programme) was infused with and, in some sense, remade by unconscious fantasy. At the same time, as a fantasy-infused intermediate space, the social practice became available for introjection, an introjection that would, in however limited a fashion, have remade Peter's internal object relations.

It is possible to argue that media texts, like other aspects of the social world, are always *mediated* by the unconscious. As we argued in Section 3.1, transference, unconscious fantasy, projection and introjection provide a 'screen' through which media texts are experienced and brought subjectively to life. However, from a psycho-social perspective, it is also the case that the unconscious is always mediated by the social. This is because unconscious experience is not said to 'lie behind' social practices and interactions, as if running parallel to them, but is constituted *within* them. They are the medium in which the unconscious, on a continual basis, comes into being. Thus, the forms of transference we identified in Peter's viewing of *Big Brother 3* can be said to have mediated his experience of the show (brought it subjectively to life for him), but, at the same time, the social practice of viewing *Big Brother* can be said to have been the medium in which Peter's unconscious was, in that moment, brought into existence and given shape.

Finally, a psycho-social perspective also suggests the ways in which the *individual and the social* might be understood as mutually constitutive. It is certainly the case that psychoanalytically informed accounts place greater emphasis on the individual than do some more sociological alternatives. The latter tend to see individuals as being equipped with particular attributes via social practices and their interactions with material objects and bodies (see, for example, Chapters 1, 3 and 4 in this volume). In contrast, as Reading 2.2 in this chapter suggested, from a psychoanalytic point of view, humans can be said to share specific capacities (such as those for transference, unconscious fantasy, projection and introjection) which are, in consequence, universal in nature and, therefore, not simply attributed to us by our social worlds. Moreover, as this chapter has sought to demonstrate, these shared capacities are said to generate a register of experience – unconscious meaning – that is distinctively individual. As suggested in Section 4.1, even where projective fantasies overlap (as they may when people share the same habitus), the individual experiences to which they give rise will not be entirely uniform. Having said this, the claim that the social is always present in the unconscious and the unconscious in the social clearly undermines any simple notion that the individual and the social denote distinct realms. As we have argued, the processes of an individual's unconscious exist only within social practices and interactions, and social practices and interactions are, in part, constituted by the unconscious processes of the individuals involved. In short, from a psycho-social perspective, the individual and the social can, to paraphrase Dawson (1994, p. 51), be thought of as 'abstracted levels of a single process'.

References

Abu-Lughod, L. (2002) 'Egyptian melodrama – technology of the modern subject?' in Ginsburg, F.L., Abu-Lughod, L. and Larkin, B. (eds) *Media Worlds: Anthropology on a New Terrain*, Berkeley, CA, University of California Press.

Bandura, A., Ross, D. and Ross, S.A. (1961) 'Transmission of aggression through imitation of aggressive models', *Journal of Abnormal and Social Psychology*, vol. 63, no. 3, pp. 575–82.

Barker, E. (2005) *Greuze and the Painting of Sentiment*, Cambridge, Cambridge University Press.

Bennett, T. (2008) 'Habit, freedom and the governance of social conduct' in McFall, E., du Gay, P. and Carter, S. (eds) *Conduct: Sociology and Social Worlds*, Manchester, Manchester University Press/Milton Keynes, The Open University (Book 3 in this series).

Big Brother 3, Channel 4 television game show. UK: Endemol/Channel 4 (2002).

Bollas, C. (1993) *Being a Character: Psychoanalysis and Self Experience*, London, Routledge.

Bourdieu, P. (1977) *Outline of a Theory of Practice*, Cambridge, Cambridge University Press.

Bourdieu, P. (1984) *Distinction: A Social Critique of the Judgement of Taste* (trans. R. Nice), London, Routledge and Kegan Paul.

Chodorow, N.J. (1999) *The Power of Feelings: Personal Meaning in Psychoanalysis, Gender, and Culture*, New Haven, CT, Yale University Press.

Dawson, G. (1994) *Soldier Heroes: British Adventure, Empire and the Imagining of Masculinities*, London, Routledge.

Freud, S. (1990 [1905]) 'Fragment of an analysis of a case of hysteria (Dora)' in Richards, A. (ed.) *Penguin Freud Library*, vol. 8, *Case Histories I* (trans. A. Strachey and J. Strachey), Harmondsworth, Penguin.

Gillespie, M. (ed.) (2005) *Media Audiences*, Maidenhead, Open University Press/ Milton Keynes, The Open University.

Gillespie, M. (2005a) 'Introduction' in Gillespie (ed.) (2005).

Gillespie, M. (2005b) 'Television drama and audience ethnography' in Gillespie (ed.) (2005).

Grossberg, L. (1992) 'Is there a fan in the house? The affective sensibility of fandom' in Lewis, L. (ed.) *Adoring Audience: Fan Culture and Popular Media*, London, Routledge.

Hochschild, A.R. (2003) *The Commercialization of Intimate Life: Notes from Home and Work*, Berkeley, CA, University of California Press.

Isaacs, S. (1952) 'The nature and function of phantasy' in Riviere, J. (ed.) *Developments in Psycho-Analysis*, London, Hogarth Press with the Institute of Psycho-Analysis.

Layton, L. (2004) 'That place gives me the heebie jeebies', *Critical Psychology: The International Journal of Critical Psychology*, issue 10, pp. 36–49.

Livingstone, S. (2005) 'Media audiences, interpreters and users' in Gillespie (ed.) (2005).

Mauss, M. (1979 [1935]) 'Techniques of the body' in Mauss, M. *Sociology and Psychology: Essays* (trans. B. Brewster), London, Routledge and Kegan Paul.

Ogden, T.H. (1979) 'On projective identification', *International Journal of Psycho-Analysis*, vol. 60, no. 3, pp. 357–73.

Ogden, T.H. (1983) 'The concept of internal object relations', *International Journal of Psycho-Analysis*, vol. 64, no. 2, pp. 227–41.

Ogden, T.H. (1994) 'The analytic third: working with intersubjective clinical facts', *International Journal of Psycho-Analysis*, vol. 75, no. 1, pp. 3–19.

Parliamentary Office of Science and Technology (1993) 'Screen violence', *The Psychologist*, August, pp. 353–6.

Screen [editorial collective] (1992) *The Sexual Subject: A* Screen *Reader in Sexuality*, London, Routledge.

The Open University (2000) D853 *Identity in question*, Study Guide Block 2, 'Psychoanalysis and psycho-social relations', Milton Keynes, The Open University.

Thomas, K. (1996) 'The psychodynamics of relating' in Miell, D. and Dallos, R. (eds) *Social Interaction and Personal Relationships*, London, Sage/Milton Keynes, The Open University.

Walkerdine, V. (1986) 'Video replay: families, films and fantasy' in Burgin, V., Donald, J. and Kaplan, C. (eds) *Formations of Fantasy*, London, Methuen.

Walkerdine, V. (1997) *Daddy's Girl: Young Girls and Popular Culture*, Houndmills, Macmillan.

Chapter 3
Boxing masculinities: attachment, embodiment and heroic narratives

Kath Woodward

Contents

1   Introduction

Figure 3.1

George Foreman fights
Muhammad Ali in the
famous fight 'Rumble
in the Jungle', 1974

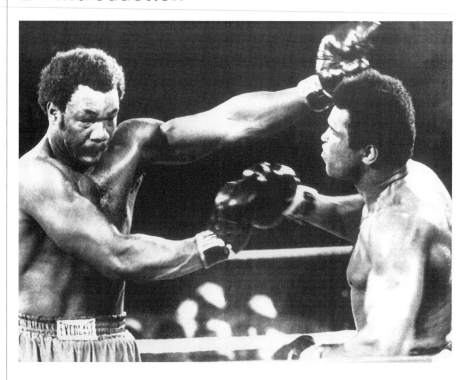

So began the third act of the fight. Not often was there a better end to
a second act than Foreman's failure to destroy Ali on the ropes. But
the last scenes would present another problem. How was the final
curtain to be found? For if Foreman was exhausted, Ali was weary. He
had hit Foreman harder than he had ever hit anyone. He had hit him
often. Foreman's head must by now be equal to a piece of vulcanized
rubber ... Ali taunts him, still the dialogue went on 'Fight hard' said
Ali, 'I thought you had some punches. You're a weak man. You're all
used up.'

... With twenty seconds left to the round, Ali attacked. By his own
measure, by that measure of twenty years of boxing, with the
knowledge of all he had learned and what could and what could not
be done at an instant in the ring, he chose this as the occasion ... he
hit Foreman with a right and left, then came off the ropes and hit
him with a left and a right ... a head-stupefying punch that sent
Foreman reeling forward ... Now Ali struck him a combination of
punches fast as the punches in the first round, but harder and more
consecutive, three capital rights in a row ... Then a big projectile
exactly the size of a fist in a glove drove into the middle of Foreman's
mind, the best punch of the startled night, the blow Ali saved for a
career. Foreman's arms flew out to the side like a man with a

parachute jumping out of a plane, and in this doubled-over position he tried to wander out to the centre of the ring ... he started to tumble and topple and fall even as he did not wish to go down ... down came the champion in sections and Ali revolved with him, in a close circle hand primed to hit him one more time.

(Mailer, 1975, pp. 199, 207, 208)

This is how the writer Norman Mailer (1975) describes Muhammad Ali's defeat of the then world heavyweight boxing champion George Foreman in the famous 'Rumble in the Jungle' in Zaire in 1974. As Mailer's account suggests, the Rumble in the Jungle – which has entered the annals of popular culture as well as boxing history – was both a spectacle of entertainment and one of raw, physical violence. Indeed, violence in boxing is inescapable and, while this may seem shocking to outsiders, it is part of what drives people's attachment to the sport.

Needless to say, the violence inherent to boxing raises interesting questions about the nature of people's attachments to it. In particular, it obliges us to ask: how do individuals become attached to a practice in which participation demands not only that you are physically violent towards your opponent but that you are yourself the object of such violence? The conventional answer to this question is that boxing provides a route out of the ghetto for impoverished and marginalised young people (Sammons, 1988). In this view, individuals box to gain self-respect and earn money. However, while economic motivations may offer a partial explanation for people's attachment to boxing, it is arguable that other, potentially more significant factors are also in play. For a start, the financial rewards are, for the vast majority of boxers, not that great. The $10 million purse that was offered for the Ali–Foreman fight as long ago as 1974 is the exception rather than the rule. More obviously, not everyone who is young and lives in the ghetto decides to box. Boxing is overwhelmingly a young *man's* pastime and, even among this group, it is only particular *individuals* who seriously engage with it. This suggests that, in order to understand how people become attached to boxing, we need to pay attention first to issues of gender (or, more specifically, masculinity) and, second, to the particular dispositions that motivate some men to step into the ring and give them the determination to stay there even when they are taking a beating.

The second of these issues – that of the boxer's 'disposition' – might suggest the need for a psychological approach to the question of the boxer's attachment to his trade. Might it be the case, for example, that boxers are of a particular psychological type, one that predisposes them to box? We might well think so, particularly when we come across evidence like that (cited in Section 3 below) of the boxer who, asked why he had not retired despite his numerous injuries, replied, 'you can't, *it's in your blood*' (Wacquant, 1995, p. 88). However, while this statement might be read as suggesting the existence of a psychological or other inherent predisposition to box, from a sociological point of view, it can be interpreted in rather different terms. As the previous chapter in this volume indicated, dispositions can be said to arise from a person's 'habitus', the specific taken-for-granted ways of orientating to the world common to a particular social group. From this point of view, our dispositions – those which guide how we more or less 'spontaneously' or 'naturally' think and act in a given situation – are viewed not as inherent psychological or biochemical states but as arising from the habits, practices, and techniques by which our bodies and minds are trained (Bourdieu, 1977; Mauss, 1979 [1935]). To be attached to boxing is, in this view, to be someone in whom the bodily and mental dispositions of the boxer have been successfully inculcated. As the chapter will argue, the training of boxer's bodies is central to this process of inculcation. Indeed, the notion of 'embodiment', which the chapter interrogates in some detail, puts into question conventional distinctions between the physical and mental. As we shall see, it is possible to argue that the bodily dispositions of the boxer are in some sense mental and his mental dispositions in some sense bodily.

In order to explore these issues, the chapter will, in Section 2, outline the Australian sociologist, Raewyn Connell's (1995) concept of 'hegemonic masculinity' and investigate its relation to boxing. In Section 3 it will move on to examine notions of embodiment and body practices via the US-based French sociologist Loïc Wacquant's ethnographic study of the boxing gym. Following on from this, Sections 4 and 5 will develop Wacquant's arguments, first in relation to gender and, second, in relation to the ways in which it can be said that social practices are enabled and constrained by the body's materiality. In so doing, Section 4 introduces the work of the feminist philosopher, Iris Marion Young, while Section 5 returns to Connell's work, specifically the concept of body-reflexive practices. The chapter's penultimate section briefly explores how boxers themselves talk about their investments in the sport and makes links back to the arguments made in the preceding sections. Finally, the Conclusion draws together the main points made in the chapter, underlining what these have to say about materiality and the relationship between the individual and the social – two of the 'sociological concerns' identified in the Introduction to this volume.

1.1 Teaching aims

The aims of this chapter are to:

■ Explore how attachments are made between individuals and the social world of sport using the particular example of boxing.

■ Establish the importance of routine, embodied practices – what people actually do with their bodies – in forging attachments within social worlds.

■ Examine matter and materiality through a focus on material bodily practices.

2   Boxing and hegemonic masculinity

Figure 3.2
Boxers embody hegemonic masculinity: Muhammad Ali fights Joe Frazier in the fight 'Thrilla in Manila', 1975

Writing in her book *On Boxing*, Joyce Carol Oates states that the sport 'is for men and is about men, and is men' (1987, p. 72). This comment is not only an empirical observation about the people who take part in boxing, but also an expression of the powerfully gendered metaphors of the sport. This is not to say that women are entirely absent from boxing. Indeed, women's boxing has a long history and, in recent years, has achieved considerable popularity, especially in the USA. Nevertheless, as the chapter Introduction argued, it is overwhelmingly men who participate in boxing and, as Mailer's account of the 'Rumble in the Jungle' illustrated, it is men's boxing which is so insistently mythologised in popular culture. (The reader should note that, because of women's relative absence from the sport and boxing's close ties with masculinity, boxers are identified throughout the chapter by the masculine pronoun 'he'.)

The mythologising that surrounds boxing – one thinks, for example, of films such as Martin Scorsese's (1980, Chartoff-Winkler) *Raging*

Bull – provides a useful point of entry into our search for an adequate explanation of the means by which the boxer becomes attached to his trade. The boxer, we can argue, in some sense embodies culturally potent ideas, beliefs and values about what it means to be a 'real' man. In her book *Masculinities* Connell (1995) described ideas, beliefs and values of this kind as constituting a 'hegemonic' version of masculinity. (It should be noted that Raewyn Connell was formerly Robert William Connell. Although *Masculinities* was written when she was still a man, an editorial decision has been taken to refer to Connell as 'she' throughout the chapter.) 'Hegemonic masculinity', she writes,

> is not a fixed character type, always and everywhere the same. It is, rather, the masculinity that occupies the hegemonic position in a given pattern of gender relations, a position always contestable.
>
> (Connell, 1995, p. 76)

As this suggests, **hegemonic masculinity** refers to the particular way of being a man that, in a given historical moment and context, successfully asserts its leadership in relation to, and authority over, both the available forms of femininity and competing versions of masculinity. To take a banal example, it is a cliché of North American 'teen' drama that the boys who are accorded the highest rank within their peer group are the 'jocks': usually white, heterosexual athletes (prototypically, members of the school's football team). As this cliché suggests, within the gender order of the North American high school, it is arguably the jocks who can most easily lay claim to being 'real men'. It is 'jock-hood' that defines what is proper and appropriate to masculinity as well as the nature of the relations between this masculinity, the available versions of femininity, and other ways of being a boy. Thus, for example, to be a girl or another type of boy (perhaps one who is 'geeky' or 'sissy') is to risk being at best the jocks' junior partner and at worst wholly subordinate to them.

As the quotation from Connell suggests, the notion of hegemony does not imply that the version of masculinity holding this position of leadership will go uncontested. Indeed, it is likely to be subject to constant challenge and, if it is to avoid being deposed, will have endlessly to assert and re-secure its authority. Equally, it is quite possible for a hegemonic masculinity to be co-opted in support of another project and thereby be given additional meanings or inflected in new ways. In fact, it is possible to argue that, as a predominantly female genre, the North American teen drama is itself engaged in just such a project. For instance, in a fairly standard storyline, the jock will discover that he has much to learn from someone – for example, a girl who is superficially unattractive or socially awkward – whom he had previously considered to be his inferior (see, for example, the 1999 romantic comedy, *She's All That*). In such moments, the hegemonic masculinity of the jock is not so much challenged as co-opted: the jock learns to be more tolerant and understanding; the girl, as often as not, learns to lighten up a little.

Applied to boxing, these arguments suggest that the sport holds a relatively privileged position as a site in which hegemonic meanings of masculinity are generated, asserted and reproduced. This is arguably true of contact sports more generally. For example, the North American sociologist Michael A. Messner has argued that contact sports are a particularly significant means by which boys and men achieve social rank involving, as they do, the collaborative rehearsal and re-enactment of a physically aggressive form of heterosexual masculinity, which he terms a 'manhood formula' (Messner, 2002, p. 123). It is also worth bearing in mind the important role that sports of all kinds play in generating cultural meanings of gender. This can be seen in the fact that women are routinely excluded from certain sports or are subject to different regulations from men. (For example, women athletes often run shorter distances and women golfers play off from tees nearer to the green.) Such differences tend to be justified in relation to issues of body size, strength and stamina (Hargreaves, 1994). However, there is little reason why men and women of similar body sizes and similar fitness and skill levels should not compete against each other. The fact that they do not would seem to tell us more about sport's role in making and reinforcing conventional understandings of gender than it does about objective differences between men and women. Nonetheless, while boxing is not the only sport that can be seen to 'make gender', as the most contact-intensive of contact sports – one in which conventional masculine attributes of physical strength, force and courage are at a premium – it can be considered to be a significant arbiter of what, in the social formations of the advanced industrialised economies, it means to be a 'real' or 'proper' man.

As the previous discussion has suggested, the fact that the boxer can be argued to embody a form of masculinity that is culturally hegemonic does not mean that this hegemony is uncontested, nor that it is incapable of being co-opted. A significant example of the latter is to be found in the fact that boxing has been a prominent site in the fight against racism. This tradition, in which Muhammad Ali is an important figure, has particular resonance in the USA (Sammons, 1988). For instance, Joe Louis's great comeback to defeat Hitler's champion, Max Schmeling, in 1938 has been described as 'a test of freedom and democracy versus Nazi philosophy and totalitarianism. It was the clearest symbolic confrontation between good and evil in the history of sport' (Hauser, 2007, p. 56). In this description, Thomas Hauser incorporates boxing into American democracy and the discourse of freedom. In effect, the boxer's ability to embody a hegemonic form of masculinity is, in this instance, co-opted to support a pro-democratic ideal of racial and ethnic tolerance. In the figure of the heroic black fighter, hegemonic masculinity becomes a vehicle for anti-racism and black pride.

As this suggests, the concept of hegemonic masculinity is useful for at least two major reasons. First, it acknowledges the cultural valorisation of the boxer and the rank that, as bearer of hegemonic masculinity, he thereby holds within the gender order. This provides a general explanation for the fact that it is men in particular who participate in and have emotional attachments to the sport. To engage in or enjoy boxing is in some sense to identify with a culturally potent emblem of masculine power. Second, as is indicated by the important role boxing has played in anti-racist struggles in the USA, the concept of hegemonic masculinity also draws our attention to the ambiguities of and opportunities for contestation and co-option inherent within hegemonic versions of gender. Viewed as the embodiment of a hegemonic form of masculinity, the boxer is not to be understood as a uniform and static entity appealing to an equally uniform and static social group (men). Instead, he is a figure who is subject to ongoing negotiation, capable of being taken up and deployed in different contexts and with different meanings. This is important because – as in the case of anti-racist struggles – it allows us to explore the ways in which masculinity intersects with other social relations (such as those of class, race and sexuality) and, in consequence, the particular resonances that boxing may have for different groups of men (and some women) in different times and places.

However, while the concept of hegemonic masculinity is clearly useful in opening up questions of how men's attachments to boxing are forged, it does not, on its own, tell us very much about how individual men come to embody forms of masculinity that are hegemonic. As the Introduction to this chapter suggested, in order to understand how men become attached to and are capable of entering a boxing ring for the purpose of hitting and being hit, we need to understand how boxing gets 'in the blood' or is constituted as a set of dispositions, something that feels natural and spontaneous. It is to these issues that the next section now turns.

3   Boxing, embodiment and body practices

In Chapter 1 of this volume it was suggested that the sexing of bodies as female or male can be seen as a social process (Butler, 1990). From this point of view, rather than the material body determining the sex it is accorded, it is the social and cultural meanings given to that body which create it as female or male; sex itself is an *inscription* upon the body which comes to be taken for granted as natural. The notion of inscription draws on the work of the French philosopher and historian, Michel Foucault (1977). As the term implies, for Foucault, bodies do not exist in some unmediated natural realm unaffected by social and political relations but are, in an important sense, the *effect* of the social meanings and practices which work upon them.

The notion of inscription has been extremely productive in drawing attention to the ways in which bodies do not simply precede the social worlds of which they are a part but are instead constituted by and through them. However, it is possible to argue that, seen in this light, bodies risk becoming little more than the passive recipients of a social world that constructs them. Is it not the case that bodies also act as well as being acted upon? Foucault was himself not unaware of this issue, arguing that bodies are not only inscribed by the social but actively participate in this inscription via *body practices*: the routines, practices, techniques and forms of training by which bodies are regulated and through which they act. Thus, for Foucault, body practices 'permit individuals to effect by their own means or with the help of others a certain number of operations in their own bodies and thought to conduct ways of being so as to transform themselves' (Foucault, 1988, p. 18).

As this suggests, if we are to understand how the boxer becomes attached to his craft – how boxing gets 'in the blood' – then, arguably, we need not only an understanding of how the boxer's body is acted upon and given meaning by the social world but also of how the boxer's body is itself active in this process. Accounts of this kind have, it is possible to argue, been most fully developed in the phenomenological tradition of sociology influenced by the work of the French philosopher, Maurice Merleau-Ponty (1962). For Merleau-Ponty, embodied experience is a central means by which the world is apprehended and imaginatively appropriated. Sociologists taking up his ideas have, in consequence, been particularly concerned to explore the extent to which the collective practices through which people make and remake their social worlds are necessarily ones that are **embodied**.

In the context of boxing, this approach has been most famously deployed by Wacquant. Wacquant's work is particularly interesting from the point of view of this chapter because it seeks to understand boxers' 'willing embrace and submission to the pain and rigour of their chosen sport' (1995, p. 88). While Wacquant acknowledges the social and economic context of boxing, he seeks to find an explanation of the processes through which boxers become part of this social world which

Figure 3.3
Ricky Hatton in the
gym: reflected glory

depends not only upon economic disadvantage. In this light, he claims
that for the boxer:

> There is an *unconscious fit between his (pugilistic) habitus and the very
> field which has produced it* ... The boxer's desire to fight flows from a
> practical *belief* constituted in and by the immediate co-presence of,
> and mutual understanding between, his (re) socialized body and the
> game.
>
> (Wacquant, 1995, p. 88; emphasis in original)

What does he mean by this? Drawing on the concept of habitus,
Wacquant argues that social groupings develop their own lasting system
of dispositions, practical beliefs and ways of doing things that are
'unconscious' in the sense of being so ingrained and taken for granted as
to appear spontaneous (Bourdieu, 1977, 1990; Mauss, 1979 [1935]). The
'boxer's desire to fight' is, then, a 'practical belief' that exists as part of
the social world or habitus of the boxer. Importantly, Wacquant alerts us
to the fact that practical belief should be understood not as a state of
mind but rather as a 'state of body' (Bourdieu, 1990, p. 68). Expanding
on this point, Wacquant writes:

> The boxer wilfully perseveres into this potentially self-destructive
> trade because, in a very real sense, he is inhabited by the game he
> inhabits. A veteran middleweight who has 'rumbled' on three
> continents for over a decade and who reported breaking his hands
> twice and his foot once, persistent problems with his knuckles
> (because of calcium deposits forming around them) as well as a
> punctured ear drum and several facial cuts necessitating stitches,

reveals this ... acceptance, made body, of the stakes of pugilism when he fails to find cause for alarm in this string of injuries: 'Sure you do think about it, but then you regroup yourself, start thinkin', you can't, it's *in your blood so much*, you can't, you been doin' it so long, you can't, you can't give it up.'

(Wacquant, 1995, p. 88; emphasis in original)

In other words, for Wacquant, the boxer fights because his body has been trained to the point where to do so has become second-nature and to do otherwise has become unthinkable.

These arguments are developed further in the following reading, taken from Wacquant's (2004) ethnographic study of a Chicago gym. (It is worth noting that Wacquant himself became a serious enough boxer to fight in the 1990 Golden Gloves amateur boxing competition.) As you read the extract, you should ask yourself: what is the process by which the boxer acquires the dispositions that allow him to fight and are these primarily mental or primarily bodily?

Reading 3.1 Loïc Wacquant, 'Body and soul: notebooks of an apprentice boxer'

To learn how to box is to imperceptibly modify one's bodily schema, one's relation to one's body and to the uses one usually puts it to, so as to internalize a set of dispositions that are inseparably mental and physical and that, in the long run, turn the body into a virtual punching machine, but an *intelligent and creative machine capable of self-regulation* while innovating within a fixed and relatively restricted panoply of moves as an instantaneous function of the actions of the opponent in time. The mutual imbrication of corporeal dispositions and mental dispositions reaches such a degree that even willpower, morale, determination, concentration, and the control of one's emotions change into so many reflexes inscribed within the organism. In the accomplished boxer, the mental becomes part of the physical and vice versa; body and mind function in total symbiosis. ...

It is this close imbrication of the physical and the mental that enables experienced boxers to continue to defend themselves and eventually rebound after skirting being knocked out. In such moments of quasi unconsciousness, their body continues to box on its own, as it were, until they regain their senses, sometimes after a lapse of several minutes. 'I went into a clinch with my head down and my partner's head came up and butted me over the left eye, cutting and dazing me badly. Then he stepped back and swung his right against my jaw with every bit of his power. It landed flush and stiffened me where I stood. Without going down or staggering, *I lost all consciousness, but* instinctively proceeded to knock him out. Another sparring partner entered the ring. We boxed three rounds. I have no recollection of this.' [1] ...

Boxers and trainers seem on first cut to hold a contradictory view of the 'mental' aspect of their activity. On the one hand, they assert that boxing is a 'thinking man's game' that they frequently liken to chess. On the other, they insist that there is no ratiocinating once you set foot in the squared circle. ... The riddle solves itself as soon as one realizes that a boxer's ability to cogitate and reason in the ring has become a faculty of his undivided organism – what John Dewey would call his 'body-mind complex'. [2]

Pugilistic excellence can thus be defined by the fact that the body of the fighter computes and judges for him, instantaneously, without the mediation – and the costly delay that it would cause – of abstract thinking, prior representation, and strategic calculation. As Sugar Ray Robinson concisely puts it: 'You don't think. It's all instinct. If you stop to think, you're gone.' An opinion confirmed by trainer Mickey Rosario: 'You can't think ... out there [in the ring]. You got to be an animal.' [3] And one must add: a *cultivated* instinct, a *socialized* animal. It is the trained body that is the *spontaneous strategist*; it knows, understands, judges, and reacts all at once. If it were otherwise, it would be impossible to survive between the ropes. And one readily recognizes novices, during amateur fights, by their rigid and mechanical moves, their slowed-down, 'telegraphed' combinations, whose stiffness and academicism betray the interventions of conscious thought into the coordination of gestures and movements.

Thus the strategy of the boxer, as product of the encounter of the pugilistic habitus with the very field that produced it, erases the scholastic distinction between the intentional and the habitual, the rational and the emotional, the corporeal and the mental. It pertains to an embodied practical reason that, being lodged in the depths of the socialized organism, escapes the logic of individual choice. ...

...

The boxer is a *live gearing* of the body and the mind that erases the boundary between reason and passion, explodes the opposition between action and representation, and in so doing transcends *in actu* the antinomy between the individual and the collective that underlies accepted theories of social action. Here again I concur with Marcel Mauss when he speaks of 'the physio-psycho-sociological assemblages of series of acts ... more or less habitual or more or less ancient in the life of the individual and in the history of the society' that are 'assembled by and for social authority.' [4]

[Notes]

[1] Former world heavyweight champion Gene Turvey, as cited in Sammons, *Beyond the Ring*, 246 (emphasis mine).

[2] John Dewey, *Experience and Nature* (Chicago, Open Court, 1929), 277.

[3] Sugar Ray Robinson is cited in Hauser, *Black Lights*, 29, and Mickey Rosario in Plummer, *Buttercups and Strong Boys*, 43.

[4] Marcel Mauss, 'Les techniques du corps', in *Sociologie et Anthropologie* (Paris, Presses Universitaires de France, 1950, orig. 1936), 368–369, trans. 'Body techniques', in *Sociology and Psychology: Essays* (London: Routledge and Kegan Paul, 1979), 120 (my translation).

Reading source

Wacquant, 2004, pp. 95–8, 17

From Wacquant's perspective, the dispositions that allow the boxer to fight – to hit and be hit – are not psychological in the sense of fixed character traits nor, despite the metaphors boxers often use to describe these dispositions, are they simply given in nature. Instead, they are inculcated in the boxer via the training regime he undergoes. In this particular extract, Wacquant does not itemise the details of this training regime but we can assume he is referring to the various body practices – sparring, working with heavy and speed punchbags, rope-skipping and so forth – by which the boxer builds strength, stamina and agility and generally develops the skills of his craft. Wacquant's point is, of course, that the boxer is only able to box effectively once, via these body techniques, boxing has become second nature to him. At this point, he will have had inculcated in him a set of dispositions which are neither purely mental nor purely physical but 'mutually imbricated' (that is, overlapping). The boxer who, in reacting to a punch thrown by his opponent, coordinates his feet, his body and his fists into a fluid and effective response, does so not as the result of conscious thought but as a *learned* 'reflex'. As this implies, this reflex is not simply instinctive. It is, instead, a kind of 'thinking with the body' in which, without the intervention of conscious thought, the boxer selects from and improvises on his repertoire of moves.

Wacquant's account is persuasive in describing the processes of embodied attachment which take place, for example, in training regimes. Boxers *are* their bodies and only become boxers through practice and physical engagement. This argument could, of course, apply to any activity in which practice is so effective that actions are carried out without reflection, such as serving in tennis or bowling in cricket. Thinking might impede the action; once you start thinking about it you fail to operate effectively. This is not to suggest that great athletes do not think or make judgements. Rather, to be effective their judgements must involve a synchrony of mind and body which ultimately eliminates the need for reflection.

However, while Wacquant's account is particularly useful in its focus on the practices of the material body, it is possible to argue that it leaves a number of questions unanswered. In particular, it seems to assume rather than explore the extent to which these practices might actively constitute hegemonic masculinity. In the light of the discussion in the previous section, we might expect him to investigate the extent to which the body that emerges in the training regimes of the boxing gym is – in terms of the way it is built, the way it is held and moves, and the skills and capacities with which it is equipped – one that is profoundly *gendered*. However, Wacquant appears relatively uninterested in this possibility. Equally, although the body is strongly present in Wacquant's account, it is possible to argue that its *materiality* is underplayed. This is to say that, while Wacquant views the dispositions inculcated in the boxer as being embodied, he pays relatively little attention to the precise ways in which they are enabled and constrained by capacities and attributes of the physical body itself. Instead, his focus tends to remain on the *social* training of the body. These issues are taken up in the following two sections. The first of these explores Young's (2005 [1975]) famous paper, 'Throwing like a girl', in which she explicitly addresses the means by which body practices can be seen as actively constitutive of gender. The second returns to the work of Connell (1995), in this instance to investigate her use of the concept of 'body-reflexive practices', one that arguably contains a stronger sense than does Wacquant's account of the body's materiality and the consequences of this.

4   Making gender

At the end of the last section, it was suggested that, although Wacquant's account draws attention to body practices as a means by which particular dispositions are inculcated in the boxer, it fails to explore the extent to which these practices actively constitute hegemonic masculinity. If the gendered dimensions of body practices are underdeveloped in Wacquant's account, we can nevertheless get some idea of what these might look like via a parallel analysis, Young's classic study, first published in 1975, 'Throwing like a girl' (Young, 2005 [1975]).

In this paper, Young demonstrates how bodies operate in space, and in the following extract she describes how this works specifically for women by examining the 'comportment' of girls (that is, their personal bearing and how this is learned). As you read, you may want to ask yourself: how do girls learn to move and carry themselves and in what ways does this help constitute gender?

Reading 3.2   Iris Marion Young, 'Throwing like a girl'

This essay ... traces in a provisional way some of the basic modalities of feminine body comportment, manner of moving, and relation in space. It brings intelligibility and significance to certain observable and rather ordinary ways in which women in our society typically comport themselves and move differently from the ways that men do. ... The account developed here claims only to describe the modalities of feminine bodily existence for women situated in contemporary advanced industrial, urban, and commercial society. [...] it is not the concern of this essay to determine to which, if any, other social circumstances this account applies.

... I concentrate primarily on those sorts of bodily activities that relate to the comportment or orientation of the body as a whole, that entail gross movement, or that require the enlistment of strength and the confrontation of the body's capacities and possibilities with the resistance and malleability of things. ...

... In accordance with [the French feminist philosopher, Simone de] Beauvoir's understanding, I take 'femininity' to designate not a mysterious quality or essence that all women have by virtue of being biologically female. It is, rather, a set of structures and conditions that delimit the typical *situation* of being a woman in a particular society, as well as the typical way in which this situation is lived by the women themselves. ... the account offered here of the modalities of feminine bodily existence is not to be falsified by referring to some individual women to whom aspects of the account do not apply, or even to some individual men to whom they do.

... [T]he basic difference ... between the ways boys and girls throw is that girls do not bring their whole bodies into the motion as much as the boys do. They do not reach back, twist, move backward, step, and lean forward. Rather, the girls tend to remain relatively immobile except for their arms, and even the arms are not extended as far as they could be. Throwing is not the only movement in which there is a typical difference in the way men and women use their bodies ... these are frequently characterized, much as in the throwing case, by a failure to make full use of the body's spatial and lateral potentialities.

...

... Many of the observed differences between men and women in the performance of tasks requiring coordinated strength, however, are due not so much to brute muscular strength as to the way each sex *uses* the body in approaching tasks. ...

The previously cited throwing example can be extended to a great deal of athletic activity. Now, most men are by no means superior athletes, and their sporting efforts display bravado more often than genuine skill and coordination. The relatively untrained man nevertheless engages in sport more generally with more free motion and open reach than does his female counterpart. Not only is there a typical style of throwing like a girl, but there is a more or less typical style of running like a girl, climbing ... , swinging, ... hitting like a girl. They have in common first that the whole body is not put into fluid and directed motion, but rather, in swinging and hitting, for example, the motion is concentrated on one body part; and second that the woman's motion tends not to reach, extend, lean, stretch, and follow through in the direction of her intention.

For many women as they move in sport, a space surrounds us in imagination that we are not free to move beyond; the space available to our movement is a constricted space. Thus, for example, in softball or volleyball women tend to remain in one place more often than men do ... Men more often move out toward a ball in flight and confront it with their own countermotion. Women tend to wait for and then *react* ...

Women often approach a physical engagement with things with timidity, uncertainty and hesitancy. ... We feel as though we must have our attention directed upon our bodies to make sure they are doing what we wish them to do, rather than paying attention to what we want to do *through* our bodies.

The three modalities of feminine motility are that feminine movement exhibits an *ambiguous transcendence*, an *inhibited intentionality*, and a *discontinuous unity* with its surroundings. A source of these contradictory modalities is the bodily self-reference of feminine comportment, which derives from the woman's experience of her body as a *thing* at the same time as she experiences it as a capacity.

... Merleau Ponty ... [locates] subjectivity not in mind or consciousness, but in the *body*. ... Now, once we take the locus of subjectivity and transcendence to be the lived body rather than pure consciousness, all transcendence is ambiguous because the body as natural and material is immanence. But it is not the ever-present possibility of any lived body to be passive, to be touched as well as touching, to be grasped as well as grasping, which I am referring to here as the ambiguity of the transcendence of the feminine lived body. ... The lived body as transcendence is pure fluid action, the continuous calling-forth of capacities that are applied in the world. Rather than simply beginning in immanence, feminine bodily existence remains in immanence or, better, is *overlaid* with immanence, even as it moves out toward the world in motions of grasping, manipulating, and so on. ... A woman frequently does not trust the capacity of her body to engage itself in a physical relation to things. ...

... Feminine existence ... often does not enter bodily relation to possibilities by its own comportment toward its surroundings in an unambiguous and confident 'I can.' ... Feminine bodily existence is an *inhibited intentionality*, which simultaneously reaches toward a projected end with an 'I can' and withholds its full bodily commitment to that end in a self-imposed 'I cannot'.

...

Merleau-Ponty gives to the body the unifying and synthesizing function that Kant locates in transcendental subjectivity. By projecting an aim toward which it moves, the body brings unity to and unites itself with its surroundings; through the vectors of its projected possibilities it sets things in relation to one another and to itself. ...

The third modality of feminine bodily existence is that it stands in *discontinuous unity* with both itself and its surrounding. I remarked earlier that in many motions that require the active engagement and coordination of the body as a whole in order to be performed properly, women tend to locate their motion in part of the body only, leaving the rest of the body relatively immobile. Motion such as this is discontinuous with itself. The part of the body that is transcending toward an aim is in relative disunity from those that remain immobile. The undirected and wasted motion that is often an aspect of feminine engagement in a task also manifests this lack of body unity. The character of the inhibited intentionality whereby feminine motion severs the connection between aim and enactment, between possibility in the world and capacity in the body, itself produces this discontinuous unity.

...

The modalities of feminine bodily comportment, [and] motility ... that I have described here are, I claim, common to the existence of women in contemporary society to one degree or another. They have their source, however, in neither anatomy nor physiology, and certainly not in a mysterious feminine essence. Rather, they have their source in the particular *situation* of women ... in contemporary society. ... There is a specific positive style of feminine body comportment and movement, which is learned as the girl comes to understand that she is a girl. ...

... At the root of these modalities ... is the fact that the woman lives her body as *object* as well as a subject. ... An essential part of the situation of being a woman is that of living the ever-present possibility that one will be gazed upon as a mere body, as shape and flesh that presents itself as the potential object of another subject's intentions and manipulations, rather than as a living manifestation of action.

Reading source

Young, 2005, pp. 30–38, 41–4

Young makes a strong case for the gender differentiation that takes place through bodily comportment and motility. Unlike Wacquant, she focuses on gender as an explicit dimension of experience. For Young, embodiment is most importantly set in particular social and cultural situations which frequently privilege masculinity. The female body, she argues, is not simply experienced as a direct communication with the active self, but is also experienced as an object. She suggests that there are distinctive manners of comportment and movement that are associated with women (hence 'throwing like a girl'). Young attributes these different modalities, first, to the social spaces in which women learn to comport themselves. In terms of sport, this involves constraints of space and learning to act in less assertive and aggressive ways than men. Second, Young suggests women are encouraged to see themselves through the gaze of others including the 'male gaze' and to become more aware of themselves as objects of the scrutiny of others.

These processes clearly have relevance for our understanding of embodied masculinity. For instance, if learning to 'throw like a girl' helps constitute an 'inhibited intentionality', it might be deduced that learning to 'throw like a boy' helps constitute forms of intentionality that are uninhibited (although we might want to note that, since boxing is a site in which those who develop attachments to available gender identities are far from privileged in relation to class, ethnicity and 'race', men who box may also suffer the inhibited intentionality to which Young refers in the other social worlds in which they participate). Viewed in this light, it is not too difficult to see how the body practices of the boxer's gym can also be understood as making gender. The ways in which the boxer learns to move and hold himself, the size and physical strength he achieves in training, and the fighting skills with which he is equipped all bespeak a hegemonic form of masculinity. In other words, via the body practices of the gym, hegemonic masculinity is, in a literal sense, made flesh.

5   Body-reflexive practices

Young's analysis clearly draws our attention to the gendered dimensions of body practices, dimensions that are arguably underplayed in Wacquant's account of the means by which boxing gets 'in the blood'. However, in Section 3, it was argued that Wacquant's argument also underplays the issue of the body's materiality. Although bodies are strongly present in his account, and are seen as active as well as acted upon, it remains the case that Wacquant is most obviously interested in the processes by which the social is 'written into' the body or 'made flesh' in the boxer's characteristic dispositions and comportment. The problem with this emphasis is that it tells us relatively little about the ways in which the materiality of the body might itself be said to enable and constrain body practices. Is it not the case, for example, that no matter how rigorous his training the skill and speed with which the boxer throws punches will decline with age?

We can address this issue by turning to a second argument from Connell's influential book, *Masculinities* (Connell, 1995). In this work, as well as advancing the notion of hegemonic masculinities, Connell develops her version of the concept of **body-reflexive practices**. At the heart of this concept is an assertion of the body's materiality and the consequentialty of this. As Connell writes, 'Bodies cannot be understood as a neutral medium of social practice. Their materiality matters. They will do certain things and not others' (1995, p. 58). The point Connell is making here is that the materiality of the body enables and constrains the work the social is able to do upon it. If we apply this argument to boxing, we could say for example that, although the ability to punch (or, at least, the ability to punch effectively in the context of a boxing match) results from rigorous training, it is *enabled* by capacities inherent to the body itself. These include, among others, the mechanism of hand to eye coordination; the ability to make a fist and to bend and extend the arm; and the ability to move the torso in such a way as to put weight behind the punch that is thrown.

As Connell (1995, p. 52) argues, the fact that the body's materiality enables and constrains the work the social is able to do upon it might be taken to suggest that the body exists in a prior relation to the social or that the social is built upon biological foundations that are in some way more important and fundamental. This, as Connell notes, is close to so-called 'sociobiological' positions in which social phenomena (such as those associated with gender) are seen as little more than outgrowths of a more fundamental and largely determining biological base (Wilson, 1978). Connell is, however, sceptical of this idea. For example, in relation to a claimed biological basis for supposedly 'male' characteristics such as aggression, she writes:

The account of natural masculinity that has been built up in socio-biology is almost entirely fictional. It presupposes broad differences in the character traits and behaviours of women and men. ... [A] great deal of research has now been done on this issue. The usual finding, on intellect, temperament and other personal traits, is that there are no measurable differences at all. Where differences appear, they are small compared to variation within either sex, and very small compared to differences in the social positioning of women and men. The natural-masculinity thesis requires strong biological determination of group differences in complex social behaviours (such as creating families and armies). There is no evidence at all of strong determination in this sense. There is little evidence even of weak biological determination of group differences in simple individual behaviours. And the evidence of cross-cultural and historical diversity in gender is overwhelming. For instance, there are cultures and historical situations where rape is absent, or extremely rare; where homosexual behaviour is majority practice (at a given point in the life-cycle); where mothers do not predominate in child care (e.g., this work is done by old people, other children or servants); and where men are not normally aggressive.

(Connell, 1995, p. 47)

If social phenomena are not determined by a pre-existing biological base, is it then the case that bodies are, in some sense, the effect of a social that precedes them as social constructionism argues (see, for example, Butler, 1990, as discussed in Chapter 1 of this volume)? Unsurprisingly, given her emphasis on the materiality of the body, Connell rejects this idea also. For Connell, social constructionist arguments, although 'wonderfully productive' (1995, p. 50), have a tendency to overemphasise the consequentiality of the social and neglect the materiality of the body. She writes:

Social constructionist approaches to gender and sexuality ... provide an almost complete antithesis to sociobiology. Rather than social arrangements being the effects of the body-machine, the body is a field on which social determination runs riot. This approach too has its leading metaphors, which tend to be metaphors of art rather than engineering: the body is a canvas to be painted, a surface to be imprinted, a landscape to be marked out ... [Yet the] surface on which cultural meanings are inscribed is not featureless, and it does not stay still.

Bodies, in their own right as bodies, do matter. They age, get sick, enjoy, engender, give birth. There is an irreducible bodily dimension in experience and practice; the sweat cannot be excluded.

(Connell, 1995, pp. 50–1)

If the biological body does not determine the social and the social does not determine the biological body, how are we to understand their relationship? Connell's answer is that they exist in a relation of *mutual constitution*. Social practices are necessarily enacted through the medium of the body and are enabled and constrained by the material dimensions of that embodiment (for example, as previously indicated, the boxer's punch – although a learned technique – is enabled by capacities inherent to the body). At the same time, as a medium through which social practices operate, the materiality of the body is itself shaped and moulded by these practices (for instance, the boxer's punch becomes increasingly powerful, faster and more accurate as it is subject to the training regimes of the gym). From this point of view, we can say (in an argument that parallels the psycho-social position adopted at the end of the previous chapter) that the materiality of the body is always present in the social and the social is always present in the materiality of the body.

Connell uses the term 'body-reflexive practices' to capture this mutually constitutive relationship. Reflexivity, in this context, refers to the property by which something bends backwards on itself. Thus, as with a central-heating thermostat which raises the air temperature and is then itself changed (switched off) when the temperature reaches the desired level, the body is, in this view, understood as something that enables and constrains social practices while, simultaneously, being altered or modified by them. Another way to understand this is to see the body and the social, not as separate entities, but as interdependent moments in a single circuit, constantly modifying each other in their mutual exchanges.

Connell's key example of the process of mutual constitution relates to one of her research respondents who described himself as sexually 'very anal orientated' (Connell, 1995, p. 60). The respondent, Don Meredith, explained how he had discovered this by chance when a young woman with whom he was having a relationship inserted her finger into his anus during sex. As Connell argues, the pleasure Don experienced in this moment was enabled by a capacity inherent to the body itself, namely the susceptibility of the 'prostate gland as well as the anal sphincters and rectal lining' to stimulation (1995, p. 61). However, this capacity did not generate Don's pleasure by itself. It was activated within a *social interaction* (Don was having sex with his girlfriend), and the *meanings* Don gave to it (that it was exciting and transgressive) derived from the meanings available to him in the social world of which he was a part. If Don had occupied another social world, perhaps a conservative religious one, he might have attributed a different meaning to the physical stimulation of his body, experiencing it, for example, as 'sinful' and therefore unpleasant or frightening. The fact that Don did attribute pleasurable meanings to this physical experience modified, in turn, his relationship to his body. Henceforth, he experienced his body as possessing a new erogenous zone. Connell's point is, of course, that this erogenous zone was neither purely physiological nor purely social. It was a hybrid, combining both the materiality of the body, social meaning and social practice in a single entity not reducible to any one of its component parts.

As this suggests, Connell's idea of body-reflexive practices provides a means of exploring the links between individuals and social worlds which accommodates material bodies. This concept redresses the problem of the 'over-social' body; that is, the body which seems entirely socially constructed at the expense of any recognition of the material, living body. These body-reflexive practices incorporate power relations as experienced through the body and the social world including its regulations and representations. Although, in discussing body-reflexive practices, Connell does not specifically address boxing, we can extrapolate from her argument to suggest that it is body-reflexive practices that constitute the social world of boxing and that, as such, the dispositions inculcated in the boxer are enabled and constrained by the body's materiality.

6   Routine masculinities: boxing and everyday life

Figure 3.4
Working out in the gym: British boxing champion Amir Khan with his trainer in 2006

How do boxers themselves explain their attachment to boxing? This reflection by a white boxer, interviewed at a gym in Sheffield in the UK as part of a research project on boxing masculinities (Woodward, 2004), is typical of many:

> Basically I were just a skinny kid at school and I used to get bashed around a bit and pushed about and I wanted to ... you know, at the same time [the heavyweight boxer] Tyson were on his way up and I used to get up at three o'clock at morning and watch Tyson. So I thought I'd give it a go. My mum weren't wanting me to box, but when I got to fifteen then I decided to give it a go and I came down and gave it a shot. I came down here because basically [local boxers] Bomber Graham were always in newspapers and Johnny Nelson, so I thought I'd give it a go. (Dave, 27)

Dave's account highlights two important aspects of the decision to 'have a go' at boxing. First, he points to his own skinny body which he identifies as the cause of his having been 'bashed around' at school. Dave's low self-esteem before he starts training in the gym is thus attributed to his body and how it is perceived by others and even before he starts boxing there is an acknowledgement that he *is* his body. As this suggests, boxing is all about bodies and especially the transformation of skinny bodies that might get 'bashed around' into fit, powerful bodies that can take care of themselves. These bodies, as both Wacquant and Young argue, can earn the respect of others through engaging in repeated, routine practices. Indeed, Dave's response illustrates the gender specificity of these body practices in a manner that has strong parallels with Young's description of the body practices and comportment of girls.

Second, in referring to the heavyweight boxer, Mike Tyson, as a heroic role model, Dave suggests the importance of hegemonic masculinity in his decision to box. Dave refers to Tyson in the period before his 1992 conviction and imprisonment for rape but, even after this, Tyson retained his heroic status in the eyes of many young men, particularly those in the black communities (O'Connor, 2002). Tyson's story doubtless demonstrates the contradictions of boxing celebrity but it is also illustrative of the persistence of attachments to a self-consciously 'tough', not to say violent, version of hegemonic masculinity, one whose reach extends beyond the boxing gym itself and into the wider cultural world. The reference to Tyson 'when he were on his way up' is also, of course, testimony to the regard in which he was held as a highly skilled, successful boxer.

As well as Tyson, Dave also refers to the local heroes, World Boxing Organisation (WBO) cruiserweight Johnny Nelson and the middleweight, Herol 'Bomber' Graham, both of whom trained at the

Figure 3.5

Former world
heavyweight
champion, Mike Tyson

same gym as he did. Dave's apparent identification with these men underlines the fact that the boxing body is, or has the potential to become, a heroic body. While boys and young men might aspire to being able to defend themselves, it is clear they also identify with successful boxing heroes and the legends and stories of boxing culture.

Although Dave does not identify this himself, one other issue is also worth mentioning here. Many young male boxers are taken to the gym by their fathers and sometimes their mothers. British lightweight Billy Schwer's experience was typical. He explains, 'My dad took me down the gym when I was eight' (*Between Ourselves*, 15 August 2006). In a similar vein, press and television coverage at the 2004 Olympics routinely showed the amateur British boxer, Amir Khan, accompanied by several members of his family. The 'naturalness' of these family attachments to boxing once again suggests that boxing makes masculinities in ways that extend far beyond the body practices of the gym and into everyday family life.

7   Conclusion

While boxing is a very distinctive social world, it presents us with a striking example of how, from a broadly phenomenological perspective, attachments can be said to be made. As the chapter has argued, boxing poses particular problems in explaining attachment because anyone participating in it faces the possibility of incurring physical damage and injury. Indeed, the point of competitive professional boxing is to cause such damage. In seeking to understand how, despite such obstacles, boxing gets 'in the blood', the chapter has argued that the boxer's capacity to fight derives not only from economic incentives or from inborn character traits but from the particular dispositions inculcated in him by the body practices of the boxing gym. While this argument is persuasively developed in Wacquant's (2004) work, the chapter has sought to extend it in a number of ways. First, via the work of Young, it has suggested that body practices make *gender*. This is important because, although not exclusively a male sport, boxing is – as was argued in Section 2 of the chapter – inextricably bound up with notions of what it means to be a 'real' or 'proper' man. Without an appreciation of the fact that boxing makes masculinity – indeed a form of masculinity that is able to lay claim to gender hegemony – we cannot grasp the profoundly gendered dimensions of the sport, the attractions this might hold for different groups of men, or the ways these play out in relation to issues of class and race. Second, via Connell's notion of body-reflexive practices, the chapter has also argued that the processes by which dispositions are inculcated are enabled and constrained by the obdurate materiality of the body. Recognition of this issue is important, the chapter has argued, because without this we will be unable to understand the hybrid 'physio-sociological' character of the dispositions inculcated in the boxer or the need to take fully into account the materiality of the body and its consequences.

As the above points indicate in exploring men's attachment to boxing, the chapter has also raised various issues related to the 'sociological concerns' identified in the Introduction to the book, in particular materiality and the relationship between the individual and the social. If the concept of body-reflexive practices alerts us to the enabling and constraining role played by the materiality of the body, it also tells us much about the relationship between the individual and the social. Most obviously, the concept suggests that individual bodies are actively shaped and given meaning by social practices. The boxer's body is, for instance, actively moulded by the body practices of the gym, gaining muscle, strength and speed. In the individual boxer's body, the social is, then, literally made flesh. However, since the individual body of the boxer is also the medium through which the social works, and since body practices are enabled and constrained by the body's materiality, it is also the case that the individual body is always present in, and actively constitutive of, the social. This is, perhaps, one of the major insights of those sociological approaches that have embodiment as their main focus of enquiry. From this point of view, the social is not a separate entity, something *made out* of body-reflexive practices and which, in consequence, follows in their wake. Instead, the social *is* these body-reflexive practices: it is their enactment and, as such, has the materiality of the body at its very heart.

References

Between Ourselves, BBC Radio 4 programme, Olivia O'Leary interviews Billy Schwer and Johnny Nelson (15 August 2006).

Bourdieu, P. (1977) *Outline of a Theory of Practice*, Cambridge, Cambridge University Press.

Bourdieu, P. (1990) *In Other Words*, Cambridge, Polity.

Butler, J. (1990) *Gender Trouble: Feminism and the Subversion of Identity*, New York, NY, Routledge.

Connell, R.W. (1995) *Masculinities*, Cambridge, Polity.

Foucault, M. (1977) *Discipline and Punish: The Birth of the Prison*, Harmondsworth, Penguin.

Foucault, M. (1988) 'Technologies of the self' in Martin, L., Gutman, H. and Hutton, P. (eds) *Technologies of the Self: A Seminar with Michel Foucault*, Amherst, MA, University of Massachussetts Press.

Hargreaves, J. (1994) *Sporting Females: Critical Issues in the History and Sociology of Women's Sports*, London, Routledge.

Hauser, T. (2007) 'The Brown Bomber is destroyed in his last ever fight', *Observer Sport Monthly*, 7 January.

Mailer, N. (1975) *The Fight*, Harmondsworth, Penguin.

Mauss, M. (1979 [1935]) 'Techniques of the body' in Mauss, M. *Sociology and Psychology: Essays* (trans. B. Brewster), London, Routledge and Kegan Paul.

Merleau-Ponty, M. (1962) *Phenomenology of Perception*, New York, NY, Routledge.

Messner, M. (2002) *Taking the Field: Women, Men, and Sports*, Minneapolis, MN, University of Minnesota Press.

Oates, J.C. (1987) *On Boxing*, New York, NY, Dolphin/Doubleday.

O'Conner, D. (ed.) (2002) *Iron Mike: A Mike Tyson Reader*, New York, NY, Thunder's Mouth Press.

Raging Bull, film, directed by Martin Scorcese. USA: Chartoff-Winkler Productions, 1980.

Sammons, J. (1988) *Beyond the Ring: The Role of Boxing in American Society*, Chicago, IL, University of Chicago Press.

She's All That, film, directed by Robert Iscove. USA: All That Productions, 1999.

Wacquant, L. (1995) 'Pugs at work: bodily capital and bodily labour among professional boxers', *Body and Society*, vol. 1, no. 1, pp. 65–93.

Wacquant, L. (2004) *Body and Soul: Notebooks of an Apprentice Boxer*, Oxford, Oxford University Press.

Wilson, E.O. (1978) *On Human Nature*, Cambridge, MA, Harvard University Press.

Woodward, K. (2004) 'Rumbles in the jungle: boxing, racialisation and the performance of masculinity', *Leisure Studies*, vol. 23, no. 1, pp. 1–13.

Young, I.M. (2005 [1975]) 'Throwing like a girl: a phenomenology of feminine body comportment, motility and spatiality' in Young, I.M. *On Female Body Experience: 'Throwing Like a Girl' and Other Essays*, Oxford, Oxford University Press.

Chapter 4
Attachment and detachment in the economy

Fabian Muniesa

Contents

1   Introduction

Imagine the following situation. It's your birthday and a friend of yours (a close one) brings over a present for you: a box of chocolates. You carefully examine the box, silently looking for the price tag or some other quantitative information (such as the weight). You set the box apart on the table. Then you open a drawer and take out a book of receipts and a pen. You tear off a receipt and start to fill it in. When you have finished, you hand it over to your friend: 'One box of chocolates, medium size. Thanks.'

Consider another hypothetical situation. You arrive home from your local supermarket. You leave your groceries in the kitchen and go straight to your computer. You open your email account and start writing: 'Dear store manager, I'm so delighted with all the lovely products that you recently gave to me! They look superb and I wanted to thank you for them all. I really want you to keep the money I gave you in return. Best regards … .'

We can probably agree that these would be rather strange situations. They are odd because they breach the ordinary logic of gift exchange and market transaction. Imagine your friend's reaction to the receipt, and the reaction of that anonymous store manager to such a letter. 'Breaching experiments' of this kind, whether imaginary (as in this instance) or real, aim to disrupt an ordinary course of action in order to reveal what normality is made of. These particular experiments expose interesting issues that arise when a good changes hands. What is really wrong with giving a receipt as a response to a gift? What does the receipt do? Why might it contradict the rules of friendship? And why would it be nonsense to write an effusive note of thanks to a store manager and to encourage her to keep the money you gave as payment for the goods purchased?

In these breaching experiments, something wrong happens to the degree of attachment and detachment that 'ought to' affect these different transfers of goods. The aim of this chapter is to explore issues of this kind using examples taken from the sociology of economic life, broadly conceived. This exploration will include the investigation of market transactions and other forms of economically relevant activity, such as gift relationships and forms of cultural consumption (specifically, listening to music) that can be seen to involve different elements, or combinations, of attachment and detachment. Here, the words 'attachment' and 'detachment' refer to relationships between persons (people may be attached to each other or detached from each other through an economic transaction), but also to relationships between persons and things (when economic goods change hands, they are successively attached to and detached from the persons they belong to). One important idea explored throughout the chapter is that attachment and detachment are both crucial processes of economic life.

As this perhaps suggests, the chapter is also attentive to a *materialistic* definition of attachments. Starting from a literal meaning of this notion, we can say that an attachment is a connection: a bond, a tie that associates two or more elements by holding them together. Things or persons that are attached to each other thus form a network, in the sense that they are articulated together. This suggests two further issues. First, elements attached in this manner are affected by each other. In other words, to exist as they are they strongly need each other: they are entangled, and this entanglement characterises them as beings. (For instance, I can say that the fact that I'm attached to such and such a thing or person affects the way I behave and also who I am.) Second, the notion of attachment calls for a deep attention to the *medium* through which the attachment is brought into being. Following a literal use of the verb 'to attach', I may say that I attach something to something else (for example, the boat to the quay) but I need to add: with something else (for example, a rope and knot). Mediation is thus a crucial component of attachment. An attachment can be performed through a wide variety of media which may include a legal bond or a contract, or a present that is given to someone as a sign of love. Detachment is an equally mediated phenomenon, and can, for instance, be enacted through a payment transfer and a receipt that guarantees that both parties to a transaction are quits.

This emphasis on 'materiality' is somewhat different from the emphases of earlier chapters in this book. In Chapter 1, for example, parent – child attachments were viewed as the outcome of social practices. In Chapter 2, people's investment in (or dislike for) media texts was seen as arising, to a significant extent, from psychological processes and the interconnection of these with social meanings and practices. In Chapter 3, men's attachment to boxing was explained in terms of the mutual constitution of social practices and human bodies. This chapter, however, will be approaching attachment and detachment as processes involving the active intervention of material objects: the exchanged things themselves (gifts, commodities) but also the wide array of artefacts that accompany the exchange process, such as the receipt or the thanks message in our imaginary breaching experiments. As already explained in the Introduction to this book, this attention to materiality is characteristic of intellectual points of view such as actor-network theory (ANT) and the anthropology of material culture.

This chapter's exploration of attachment and detachment begins, in the next section, by focusing on the cultural consumption of music. The aim here will be to examine some of the theoretical and methodological implications of different sociological approaches to processes of attachment. Looking in particular at the work of two French sociologists, Pierre Bourdieu and Antoine Hennion, the section explores what is at stake in people's preferences for and appreciation of different styles of music. The chapter then moves on, in Section 3, to investigate some classic anthropological discussions of gift exchange. These are particularly useful in helping us understand the way in which the circulation of objects may link together mutually obliged persons. Section 4 develops these arguments by exploring how an object may be marked and personalised so as to promote attachment. Next, Section 5 investigates how, in market transactions, despite the fact that payment is assumed to cancel reciprocal obligations between parties and to alienate goods from their original owners, there may still exist variable compromises between attachment and detachment. The chapter's penultimate section focuses on several further examples of detachment and attachment devices that help explain how economic exchange is constructed, and the conclusion draws out the implications of the preceding argument for our understanding of two of the 'sociological concerns' identified in the Introduction to this book: materiality and mediation.

1.1 Teaching aims

The aims of this chapter are to:

- Explore processes of attachment and detachment in the sociology of economic life.

- Introduce key theoretical aspects of the anthropological analysis of economic exchange.

- Discuss several empirical examples of attachment and detachment devices and promote a sociological reflection on these.

- Suggest the relevance of a materialistic approach to the study of economic situations and processes.

- Extend our understanding of materiality and mediation as sociological concerns.

2   Consumption and the love of music

Let's begin our examination of how people get attached to something by looking at a particular example: the cultural consumption of music and the formation of musical taste. Music is a global industry (we frequently refer to the 'music industry' to cover the whole gamut of recorded music from classical to world music) and yet the love of music appears to be a very personal matter. The production and consumption of music, or musical taste in general, therefore offers an interesting case study for anyone interested in the sociology of attachment.

Explanations of musical attachment often waver between quite opposing perspectives. The aesthetic properties and objective qualities of the musical work are frequently evoked as major reasons for attachment. Other explanations, however, argue that musical taste is a subjective matter and that there is little in sound itself that can explain why someone likes or dislikes a particular piece of music. Attachment, from this point of view, might thus be considered to be psychologically contingent; that is, dependent on an individual's personal inner world or their strategies of self-presentation in everyday life. A third set of explanations, properly sociological, would tend to examine the social determinations of attachment; that is, the extent to which personal dispositions depend on socialisation processes and social origins. In these explanations, the context of education becomes crucial for the understanding of musical preferences. As suggested in Chapter 2, the work of Bourdieu stands as a major contribution in this area. In his famous book *Distinction*, Bourdieu (1984) examines the correspondence between social positions and personal dispositions in matters of taste. The distinction between a 'popular' and a 'legitimate' taste, he argued, appears to be the result of a social game of which actors are not completely conscious. From this perspective, although it would be hard to deny that the feeling someone attaches to Henry Purcell's *King Arthur* or to the punk rock band The Clash's 'London Calling' is a matter of personal taste, it would also be possible to focus on statistical regularities that would link listeners of each to rather differentiated social statuses (although, nowadays, a liking for the music of The Clash probably has more sophisticated connotations than previously). This kind of analysis becomes even more evident if we tackle differences in musical preferences among different cultural communities. For example, I might have a genuine taste for flamenco music, but the fact that I am of Spanish origin could provide an external, sociological clue to explain this attachment.

Linking musical taste to external causes such as the social trajectory or the cultural background of the listener is an interesting way to expose the social logic of cultural consumption. But this type of analysis is of little help in understanding what actually *happens* in the moment of listening. There are dozens or even hundreds of ways of being attached to the music of Henry Purcell or The Clash. Flamenco can be experienced in many forms, even for the culturally labelled 'Spanish gipsy' musician. How can this variety of attachment experiences be captured? Other sociological strategies are possible that put aside external determinations and instead consider attachment as a singular accomplishment; that is, as an irreducible, unique experience (an experience that, as a result, cannot be said to be, in any straightforward fashion, determined by external social factors). One example of such a strategy can be found in the work of Hennion. In his ethnographic and historiographic studies of music lovers, Hennion (Hennion, 1997, 2001, 2004; see also Gomart and Hennion, 1999) focuses on persons who have a passionate relationship to music, either as listeners or as amateur musicians. In this work, he tries to avoid excessive sociologism (of the kind that might be associated with Bourdieu), by concentrating on how attachments are expressed. For instance, when carrying out fieldwork interviews he purposefully restrains interviewees from engaging in (often spontaneous) self-analysis of their own sociological determinations and, instead, asks them to just say 'what happens' when they listen to or play music.

As this suggests, the perspectives advocated by Bourdieu and Hennion are quite different. In fact, they even advocate rather different roles for the sociologist. Bourdieu, for example, tends to develop critical analyses, as is apparent in the following:

> The members of the different social classes differ not so much in the extent to which they acknowledge culture as in the extent to which they know it. Declarations of indifference are exceptional, and hostile rejection even rarer – at least in the legitimacy-imposing situation set up by a cultural questionnaire reminiscent of an examination. One of the surest indications of the recognition of legitimacy is the tendency of the most deprived respondents to disguise their ignorance or indifference and to pay homage to the cultural legitimacy which the interviewer possesses in their eyes, by selecting from their cultural baggage the items which seem to them closest to the legitimate definition, for example, works of so-called light music, Viennese waltzes, Ravel's *Bolero*, or some great name more or less timidly pronounced.
>
> (Bourdieu, 1984, p. 318)

In other words, Bourdieu argues that the sociologist must 'see through' the participants' response to the social categories that lie behind it. In contrast, observe how Hennion's perspective challenges the sociologist's critical position assumed in Bourdieu's analysis. Here is what he says about his way of conducting research:

> Another idea guiding the inquiry was that it was possible and necessary to 'free' discourse – not only with the sociologist but also and above all with the interviewee – on the music lover's practices, pleasures and love, from the weight under which the sociology of taste has crushed them by denouncing these emotions as cloaking a social game of which the actors are not aware. We need to assess

the destructive effects of the popularization of this form of sociology, which determines the way sociologists are received. Music lovers immediately feel guilty, suspected; they are ashamed of their pleasure, they decode and anticipate the meaning of what they say, accuse themselves of a practice that is too elitist, and over-admit the ritual nature of their rock outings or love for opera. Worse still, they no longer talk of objects, gestures, their feelings, the uncertainties that make the difficult career of the aficionado so charming. Instead, they put themselves in the categories they suppose are being held out for them and have only one concern: not to appear unaware of the fact that their taste is a sociological question. People are now so 'sociologized' that when you ask them what their musical tastes are, they will begin by apologizing: 'my family was very middle-class, I was taught by a private tutor, my sister played the violin ...'. Quite apart from the important, but not exclusive, question of the social determinants that influence taste, in the shallow receptacle created by this negative sociology of taste, it is vital to understand what it means to 'like something' nowadays, how it is experienced, what medium is used and with whom it takes place.

(Hennion, 2001, p. 5)

The 'pragmatic' sociology defended by Hennion (the label that he uses to define his approach, one very close to ANT) is quite different from Bourdieu's 'critical' sociology (for further details on this opposition in contemporary French sociological theory, see Bénatouïl, 1999). It is interested in *what* people do and *how* they do this, not in 'seeing through' these to what 'might lie behind them'. But what does Hennion's point of view tell us about attachment? Three main insights can be taken from his argument.

The first is that attachment to music is particularly tricky to analyse in terms of agency. It is, in fact, a context in which usual notions of purpose and freedom of action become extremely blurred since to love music means to be 'affected' or 'moved' by it – something that acknowledges the agency or strength of the *thing* that affects or moves us. As this suggests, Hennion sets out to challenge the usual point of view according to which freedom is almost synonymous with independence and detachment, whereas ideas of attachment and dependence convey a sense of submission or subjection. For Hennion, to be constituted as a person (a 'passionate listener' in the case of music) is precisely to be attached to something.

The second insight that is emphasised by Hennion is that the love of music has the characteristics of a performance. The expression or enactment of musical attachments depends on the meticulous care with which music lovers construct a space devoted to personal listening.

Music is a passion but listening is not purely passive as it implies a number of gestures that are necessary for the preparation of a felicitous experience. These gestures, actions and rituals include elements such as the selection and the organisation of listening materials and equipment, but also corporeal expressions of the motion of music itself. Such gestures can be of many sorts. They can, for example, be collective, as would be the case of fans dancing in the 'mosh pit' in front of the stage at a rock concert. Alternatively, they can be purely individual, as might be the case of someone 'conducting' his favourite classical symphony in the privacy of his sitting room.

The third insight Hennion points to is the crucial role of mediation in musical attachments. Musical experience is mediated by a myriad of objects and devices, starting with musical instruments themselves but also including recording and phonographic equipment. The rise and development of radio and recorded sound in the twentieth century have allowed for the emergence of a new type of listening experience and, accordingly, of a new type of listener who can benefit from an intimate contact with music, away from the sites of musical performance (concert halls or other musical gatherings). Interestingly, the accumulation of such musical mediators does not translate into a feeling of distance and estrangement but often into a feeling of immediacy. Think for instance of all the music lovers who feel that recordings, headphones and MP3 players bring them 'closer' to music than the practice of direct, public performance. Paradoxically, the more mediated it is, the more 'authentic' the listening experience can be.

This section has pointed to at least two sociological strategies that are possible in the study of attachment, one being a critical analysis of the social determinants of individual preferences and the other an ethnographic examination of the materiality of attachment as an idiosyncratic experience. As suggested in the chapter Introduction, it is the latter strategy, and the approaches allied to it, that are the primary interest of this chapter. With this in mind, these ideas can now begin to be applied to an analysis of attachments in economic transactions proper.

3   Gifts and obliged persons

An important body of literature that provides us with some crucial instruments for understanding the complex processes of entanglement between persons and things is that surrounding the 'anthropology of the gift'. Gift rituals and gift economies constitute a privileged object of anthropological enquiry, in part because they constitute an interesting counterpoint to our contemporary market-based societies. What can we learn about attachments from this literature? When a precious good is given away, attachment is at stake between the giver and the receiver, and between them both and the given object. A detour through gift giving in so-called 'archaic' societies can thus help us understand a central feature of the construction of social worlds: how people remain attached and obliged to each other through the circulation of 'attaching' objects.

A crucial text in the anthropological literature is *The Gift* published in 1924 by the eminent French anthropologist and sociologist Marcel Mauss (for a translation see Mauss, 1990 [1924]). In his essay, Mauss observes that in many ethnographic accounts of 'archaic' societies where **gift exchange** plays an important ritual or economic role, a threefold pattern can be identified. First, in these societies there seems to exist an obligation to give: in order to have a successful social existence, people need to make gifts to each other or to divinities. Second, there is an obligation to receive: it is a convention that gifts should not be refused. Third, there is an obligation to give back: within a convenient time span, every gift is followed by a counter-gift. The gift thus seems to favour the building of a social world populated by obliged persons; that is, persons entangled within reciprocal duties. But what creates these obligations? What in the gift obliges us to give, to receive and, more importantly, to give back? Anthropologist Maurice Godelier talks about the 'enigma of the gift' to refer to this anthropological question (Godelier, 1999). This enigmatic obligation can be formulated in terms of attachment: how can the gift create a bond between the giver and the receiver? Anthropological evidence on this question converges on a single point: the receiver is still obliged to the giver because the object the receiver holds is still attached to the giver. We can see this if we focus more narrowly on some classical anthropological examples.

In his celebrated essay, Mauss pointed to a remarkable correspondence between gift rituals in different, distant cultures. In gift exchange among the Maori in Polynesia, for example, the gift (called *taonga*) is said to carry a spirit (the *hau*) and to provide power (*mana*) to the one holding or possessing it. As Mauss explained, the Maori's believe that, when put into circulation, the spirit of the gift seeks to come back to its original owner. Mauss thought that this twofold principle of the *mana* (the power provided by the gift) and the *hau* (the spirit of the gift seeking to come back to its origin) was a key element that could be identified in other gift cultures, and hence explain the obligation of the gift. In his essay, he drew some resemblance between the Maori *mana* and *hau* and, for instance, the *kula* exchange, a ritual gift exchange found in Melanesia and first described by the anthropologist Bronislaw Malinowski.

The *kula*, an extremely complex gift-exchange ritual that takes place between the inhabitants of the Trobriand Islands in the Melanesian archipelago, involves the circulation of necklaces (*soulava*) and armlets (*mwali*) that literally travel from island to island, in opposite directions,

Figure 4.1

The circulation of objects in the *kula* exchange. The original figure from which this map is taken notes that it shows the area, trade routes and communities of the circular exchange. The dotted circles represent the *Kula* communities; the dotted squares represent the districts indirectly affected by the *Kula*

describing a 'ring' or *kula* (see Figure 4.1) (Malinowski, 1920, 1922). The possession of *soulava* or *mwali* confers power and prestige. But these presents cannot be held for long. They need to be given away and thrown again into the exchange ring, so as to circulate and thus increase their value. More contemporary accounts of the *kula* exchange provided by anthropologists such as Annette Weiner (1976) have identified what happens at the extremities of the ring. Each item that has circulated in the *kula* ends up in the hands of the person who first initiated it months or even years before. This person is the artisan who actually manufactured the necklace or armlet in question. These objects, it would seem, actually belong to that individual. They are his personal property, his *kitoum*. The *kitoum* has thus come back to its original owner at the end of a long chain of ritual presents.

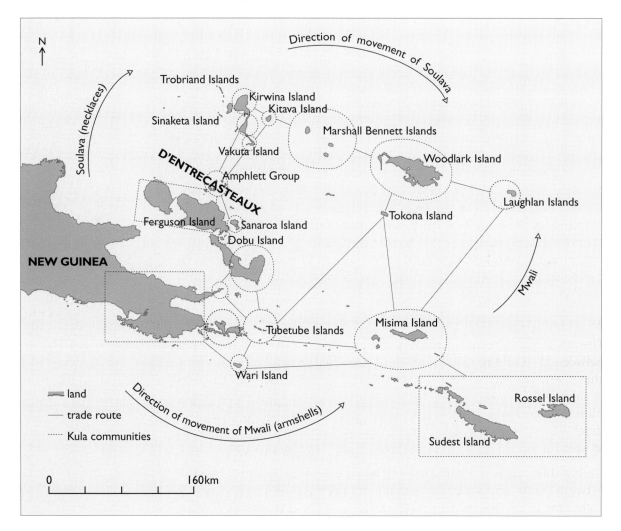

Mauss's emphasis on 'the spirit of the gift' has been subject to some criticism, for instance by the anthropologist Claude Lévi-Strauss who thought it was a somewhat mystical explanation and thus not properly scientific. But Godelier has shown that Mauss's intuition was not so flawed (Godelier, 1999; but see also Thomas, 1991). The spirit of the given thing is not, Godelier argues, a mysterious force but, more prosaically, the way in which the original owner is made present in the gift. The reason why in these 'archaic' societies the gift (or its corresponding counter-gift) is 'pushed' to return to its original owner is that it is not completely alienated from him. The giver and the receiver are not quits – that is, they remain bound to each other – because the given object is not completely detached from the giver. Although the receiver possesses the gift and can enjoy it to some extent, the gift does not belong to him completely. He cannot destroy it and he cannot keep it for too long. Instead, he must set it in motion again.

In the following extract, Godelier summarises the anthropological intuition according to which gifts construct bonds between 'obliged' persons, and emphasises how this helps create social order. As you read, you may want to note the ways in which the form of social order that is created can be more or less benign.

Reading 4.1   Maurice Godelier, 'The enigma of the gift'

In explanation of why people give, Mauss ... postulates that *what creates the obligation to give is that giving creates obligations*. To give is voluntarily to transfer something that belongs to you to someone who you think cannot refuse to accept it. The donor can be a group or an individual acting on his own behalf or on that of a group. Likewise, the recipient can be an individual or a group or someone who receives the gift as a representative of a group.

...

The act of giving seems to create simultaneously a twofold relationship between giver and receiver. A relationship of *solidarity* because the giver shares what he has, or what he is, with the receiver; and a relationship of *superiority* because the one who receives the gift and accepts it places himself in the debt of the one who has given it, thereby becoming indebted to the giver and to a certain extent becoming his 'dependant', at least for as long as he has not 'given back' what he was given.

Giving thus seems to establish a difference and an inequality of status between donor and recipient, which can in certain instances become a hierarchy: if this hierarchy already exists, then the gift expresses and legitimizes it. Two opposite movements are thus contained in a single act. The gift decreases the distance between the protagonists because it is a form of sharing, and it increases the social distance between them because one is now indebted to the other. It is easy to see the formidable array of maneuvers and strategies virtually contained in the practice of gift-giving, and the gamut of contradictory interests that can be served. By its very nature, gift-giving is an ambivalent practice which brings together or is capable of bringing together opposing emotions and forces. It can be, simultaneously or successively, an act of generosity or of violence; in the latter case, however, the violence is disguised as a disinterested gesture, since it is committed by means of and in the form of sharing.

Reading source

Godelier, 1999, pp. 11–12

As this reading indicates, anthropological studies of 'archaic' societies show that the circulation of objects in gift exchange creates bonds between persons who remain in the debt of each other. The next section will explore how objects themselves play a crucial, material role in the achievement of this process of attachment.

4 Marked objects

How does a circulating object become a vehicle for attachment? Through which medium? Going back to our earlier discussion of the 'spirit of the gift' in 'archaic' gift exchange, we can pose this question in the following way: how is the presence of the giver contained in the gift so that the receiver can recognise, in the object, their obligation towards the giver? One key factor here is the personalisation of the gift, or even its personification. In 'archaic' gift exchanges such as the ones mentioned in the preceding section, circulating gifts are personified. In the *kula* exchange, for instance, the circulating objects (the *mwali* and the *soulava*) are considered to be alive and to behave as gendered persons. In more contemporary instances of gift exchange, the personalisation of gifts continues to be an important ingredient of gift-giving etiquette. When we make a gift, we tend to personalise it; that is, to accompany it with signs (for instance, a handwritten personal card) that denote personal presence. Conversely, when we talk about a gift we received, the personal element is still present: we usually say 'this is from that person' rather than just saying 'this is mine' (we do not talk about objects in the same manner if we have purchased them ourselves). Of course, in contemporary societies there exist purely altruistic forms of gift giving that can be (and often tend to be) anonymous. Anonymity may even be a crucial element in health-related gifts such as blood or organ donation (Titmuss, 1970). Does this means that the gift becomes impersonal? Not quite, if we consider the importance of elements of communication that surround blood and organ donation (publicity campaigns, donor cards, etc.) and emphasise the personal commitment and social 'obligation' attached to the act, even if this is not directed towards specific individuals.

In fact, the donor card provides an example of the importance of what we might term **attachment devices**, in situations in which personalisation or personification is not straightforward. It is not the same thing to sell blood and get a receipt as it is to give blood and get a donor card with our name and photograph on it. The donor card links us to a community of (mutually obliged) persons and makes us aware of our duty to give further. In contrast, a receipt would mean that we were 'quits': that we would have no further obligation to give. Donor card; receipt: these are the kinds of 'devices' that allow us to identify whether particular situations are largely on the side of attachment, largely on the side of detachment, or combine both.

Economic sociologist Viviana Zelizer has focused on the analysis of these kinds of devices in her historical investigations of money. Money is said to be an extremely impersonal and abstract object. But, then, what happens with money gifts? Is there a way we can talk about the personalisation or the personification of money? Zelizer uses this extreme case in order to detect the features that allow the transformation of money into a gift. In her book *The Social Meaning of Money* (Zelizer, 1997), she studies the etiquette of money gift giving in early twentieth-century North American culture. She is particularly attentive to the ways in which some situations require that money be personalised.

For example, a crucial point that Zelizer focuses on is something called 'earmarking' (see Figure 4.2). To earmark means to mark down or to tag, but also to allocate or assign. A banknote that is earmarked as a gift is likely to create certain moral obligations in the receiver. Imagine the following example: a granddaughter receives a £10 banknote from her grandmother. The banknote is new, and is folded in an envelope on which the name of the granddaughter is handwritten. The grandmother says to her granddaughter, 'Here, this is for you to go out with your boyfriend.' Will the granddaughter dare to use this money for, say, groceries? Well, she can, of course. But even if she dares to use this precise banknote for other purposes, the next time she goes out with her boyfriend she may nevertheless treat them both with £10 on behalf of her grandmother. In any case, something has been done in order to create some kind of obligation: an obligation that stems from the fact that the person who gives is still present, through earmarking, in the given object (which is called, precisely, a 'present').

Figure 4.2

'Earmarking' a banknote ensures the giver is still present in the gift

To my Granddaughter Amie

In another example, taken from her later book *The Purchase of Intimacy* (2005), Zelizer pursues her investigation of money and personal entanglement. In this instance, she is interested in the transfer of money between intimate counterparties. For example, a situation where a sexual exchange between two persons is followed by a transfer of money can be interpreted in many ways. Was the money a payment? Or was it a treat, a mark of love? Zelizer is interested in situations in which lovers themselves disagree on the interpretation of the relation – situations of mutual accusation that can very well end up in court (fiscal authorities can be interested in obtaining a precise characterisation of the transfer, in order to determine if taxes are due). What Zelizer shows is that, in the North American court cases she documented, earmarking or personalisation of money may play a crucial role in determining the nature of the relation. Was it a relationship of attachment, or one of detachment? The marking and earmarking of money can serve as evidence of the nature of the relation. Imagine that an extramarital relation between a man and a woman is repeatedly punctuated by transfers of money. The economic gesture can very well be interpreted as a payment, and the situation as one of prostitution. But if money is accompanied by a love letter, the situation is different. Money is not then transferred in order for the two counterparties to be quits, but as a way of making affection explicit (and the relationship alive). In economic terms, the transfer is identical in both cases. But from the point of view of material culture, and in respect of attachment, we are confronted with very different cases.

In the following extract, Zelizer describes a particularly ambiguous situation of this kind. As you read, you may want to identify the precise mechanisms for attachment and detachment that appear to have been in play and consider the extent to which the transfer of money fell on the side of one or the other.

Reading 4.2 Viviana Zelizer, 'The purchase of intimacy'

David Kritzik, a wealthy widower, 'partial to the company of young women', had over the course of at least six years given Leigh Ann Conley and Lynnette Harris, twin sisters, more than half a million dollars, in kind and cash: he regularly left a check at his office, which Conley picked up every week to ten days either from Kritzik himself or from his secretary (*United States v. Harris* 942 F.2d 1125, 1128 (7th Cir. 1991)).

The case raises the issue of the taxability of monetary transfers to a mistress in long-term relationships. Were those transfers gifts or compensation? If gifts, Kritzik had to pay gift tax on the money; if compensation, the sisters had to pay income tax. The United States claimed that the money was compensation. As part of its evidence, the government argued that the form of transfer, a regular check, was that of an employee picking up wages. Sisters Harris and Conley were convicted of evading income tax obligations and sent to jail. After Kritzik's death, however, their attorneys appealed the case. Although the government insisted that the form of monetary transfer identified it as compensation, the appeal pointed out that it could have been an entitlement: 'this form of payment ... could just as easily be that of a dependent picking up regular support checks' (1129). The district court, furthermore, rejected an affidavit presented by Kritzik to Internal Revenue Service investigators before his death, in which he stated that both Harris and Conley were prostitutes. The court dismissed his claim as a likely lie to protect himself from civil or criminal penalties for his failure to pay gift taxes.

The court finally agreed that Kritzik's payments were gifts. Invoking legal precedent, the appellants' counsel successfully argued that 'a person is entitled to treat cash and property received from a lover as gifts, as long as the relationship consists of something more than specific payments for specific sessions of sex' (1133–34). A number of Kritzik's letters to Harris entered the trial record as evidence of his continuing affection and trust. He wrote, for instance, that 'so far as the things I give you are concerned – let me say that I get as great if not even greater pleasure in giving than you get in receiving,' adding, 'I love giving things to you and to see you happy and enjoying them' (1130). In another letter, he told Harris, 'I ... love you very much and will do all that I can to make you happy' (1130), adding that he would take care of Harris's financial security.

What was appellants' counsel doing? The appeal challenged the idea that economic transactions speak for themselves, as well as the effort to deduce relations from transactions alone. Indeed the judges in the case negotiated over exactly where to place the boundary of commercial and loving relationships. Judge Flaum, while concurring in the reversal of the sisters' convictions, worried about the breadth of the principle that his fellow judges invoked: 'I part company with the majority when it distils from our gift/income jurisprudence a rule that would tax only the most base type of cash-for-sex exchange and categorically exempt from tax liability all other transfers of money and property to so-called mistresses or companions' (1135).

Reading source

Zelizer, 2005, pp. 96–8

As this suggests, although money was folded into an envelope and picked up in a rather impersonal manner, a set of love letters accompanied these transfers, providing evidence of gift giving. This and other examples examined in this section show that earmarking and personalisation of exchanged objects serve as vehicles for attachment. In the next section, we shall observe a concomitant process of detachment that characterises market transactions.

5   Being 'quits' and being 'embedded'

The following dialogue occurs at the beginning of Francis Ford Coppola's film *The Godfather* (Paramount, 1972). One of the characters, Bonasera, has asked Don Corleone to take revenge against the men who have attempted to rape his daughter:

Don Corleone: *Why did you go to the police? Why didn't you come to me first?*

Bonasera:	*What do you want of me? Tell me anything, but do what I beg you to do.*
Don Corleone:	*What is that? [Bonasera whispers his request in the Don's ear] That I cannot do.*
Bonasera:	*I will give you anything you ask.*
Don Corleone:	*We've known each other many years, but this is the first time you ever came to me for counsel or for help. I can't remember the last time that you invited me to your house for a cup of coffee, even though my wife is godmother to your only child. But let's be frank here. You never wanted my friendship. And uh, you were afraid to be in my debt.*
Bonasera:	*I didn't want to get into trouble.*
Don Corleone:	*I understand. You found paradise in America, you had a good trade, you made a good living. The police protected you and there were courts of law. And you didn't need a friend like me. But, uh, now you come to me and you say: 'Don Corleone, give me justice'. But you don't ask with respect. You don't offer friendship. You don't even think to call me Godfather. Instead, you come into my house on the day my daughter is to be married, and you, uh, ask me to do murder for money.*
Bonasera:	*I ask you for justice.*
Don Corleone:	*That is not justice. Your daughter is still alive.*
Bonasera:	*Let them suffer then, as she suffers. How much shall I pay you?*
Don Corleone:	*Bonasera, Bonasera. What have I ever done to make you treat me so disrespectfully? If you'd come to me in friendship, then this scum that ruined your daughter would be suffering this very day. And if by chance an honest man like yourself should make enemies, then they would become my enemies. And then they would fear you.*
Bonasera:	*Be my friend. Godfather. [Bonasera bows toward the Don and kisses the Don's hand]*
Don Corleone:	*Good. Someday, and that day may never come, I'll call upon you to do a service for me. But, uh, until that day – accept this justice as a gift on my daughter's wedding day.*
Bonasera:	Grazie, *Godfather.*

(transcription by chapter author)

This conversation is interesting because of the way Don Corleone insists that Bonasera's request be governed by the logic of the gift rather than that of a commercial transaction. Bonasera would prefer to pay rather than remaining in the Godfather's debt. But Don Corleone's power is precisely based on a network of 'generous' obligations. He explicitly prefers to provide the service as a gift. The gift operates as a sign of friendship, even kinship, since, in calling Don Corleone his 'Godfather', Bonasera accepts the rights and responsibilities of a member of the 'family'. Consequently, the gift also operates as a guarantee that an equivalent counter-gift will be provided when it is asked for.

As this example suggests, a world full of reciprocal obligations will not always be one that entails benign forms of social solidarity. The social world created by reciprocal obligations can sometimes be one that is hostile and even murderous, as is brilliantly exemplified in Coppola's film. This is equally apparent from the anthropological literature. As is explained at length by Mauss (1990 [1924]), gift exchange can be agonistic – that is, governed by a logic of hostility and rivalry. Such is the case of the *potlatch*, an important gift institution first studied by the eminent anthropologist Franz Boas among the Kwakiutl on the north-western coast of North America, in which the purpose of the gift is to humiliate its receiver, to overwhelm them with a gift so grandiose that they will never succeed in responding to it. In the *potlatch* an obligation to counter-giving is created and, if possible, maintained by the giver as a sign of this individual's power and worth.

The problems that can result from exchanges based on reciprocal obligations underline the importance of devices that allow people to 'be quits'; that is, to no longer remain in each other's debt. This is what happens in **market exchange**. When a good changes hands in the marketplace, a concomitant transfer of money allows the effective unwinding of reciprocal obligations. Schematically speaking, a thing that is transformed into a commodity and exchanged against payment is a thing that has been properly detached from the original owner, who, by definition, does not have any remaining right over it (Muniesa, 2005). It is then attached to its new owner, and becomes part of the recipient's world. When we talk about two persons who exchange something and succeed in cancelling, through agreed payment, the reciprocal duties engendered in transfer, we can say that, as commercial counterparties in this precise transaction, they are detached from each other in the sense that they are 'quits' and no longer remain in each other's debt. Equally, once the transaction has been concluded, the object bought and sold – now a commodity – no longer belongs to its former owner. A complete transfer of property has taken place and the new owner can take full advantage of the object. The good has been 'alienated' from its original owner (the object no longer belongs to that person). The seller detaches from it, and it is now the buyer who is attached to it.

This process of detachment is clearly important in disentangling people and goods as well as disentangling people from each other. However, in real market situations, detachment is often combined with multiple processes of attachment and reattachment. Some commodities may not, for instance, be fully alienated or detached even when securely located in commercial circuits. For example, when I buy a book from a bookseller it certainly becomes mine in the sense that I am able to keep it on my bookshelf, give it away as a present, resell it to a second-hand bookstore, or even destroy it. However, there are limits to my 'ownership' of the book. For instance, I cannot copy its content or put my name on it as its author in order to sell it. I cannot even quote from it in these terms. In other words, although I own the book as such, I am not the owner of some part of it: its 'content'. The author, or the editor, or publisher, is still, in some sense, the owner of the words and sentences that constitute intellectual property. And because this composite ownership is acknowledged by law and marked in the object itself (the book is 'by' its author, and there is a copyright notice), the commodity is not completely alienated, disentangled. Such issues of intellectual property provide interesting examples of goods that have entered the realm of commodities but nevertheless behave (in some aspect, and with many nuances) like the Maussian gift, marked as they are with the name of the person to which the good is still (partially) attached.

Similar nuances appear when we deal with the detachment of commercial counterparties. In empirical market situations, once commercial counterparties have closed a transaction, they may very well still be socially attached to each other. They may, for instance, still belong to the same social network and may know each other and have personal relations as well as purely commercial ones. This can complicate the disentangling process. For example, the seller may, at a later date, feel obliged to purchase something from the buyer (rather than another, perhaps cheaper, supplier) simply because the buyer had previously been 'generous' enough to buy something from the seller.

In fact, as economic sociologists such as Mark Granovetter have shown, commercial transactions often depend on the pre-existence of social networks in which the potential counterparties to a trade are already in contact with each other, attached by a set of social obligations such as the ones implied by kinship (Granovetter, 1985, 1995). This phenomenon is often referred to as 'embeddedness'. Using examples taken from the work of anthropologist Clifford Geertz (1963) on the effect of kinship solidarities in the emergence of market entrepreneurship in Indonesia, Granovetter (1995) demonstrates how or less explicitly, to get the customer tied to a product, to a brand or to a shop. As such, they constitute an integral part of the history of mass consumption (Strasser, 1989; Tedlow, 1989; McFall, 2004; Hennion and Méadel, 1989; Cochoy, 1998).

Some aspects of these arts of attachment are related to the anthropological features that were examined in earlier sections in this chapter. In the light of the earlier discussion of gifts (in Sections 3 and 4), it is not surprising that gifts themselves play an important role as merchandising devices, in the form of, for example, coupons, promotional items and special vouchers. And what about brands? Wouldn't it be possible to interpret the presence of the brand in the commodity in the light of the 'spirit of the thing' (the Maori *hau*, the Trobriandese *kitoum*)? Of course, branded commodities are not gifts. But the emphasis on attachment (to such and such brand) is not completely unrelated to the idea of having the original manufacturer symbolically present in the object we buy. Indeed, the very notion of the 'brand' (which originally referred to a mark of ownership by 'branding') conveys the idea of the mark of the original owner or producer to whom the good is still somehow attached.

Of course, once purchased, the branded good changes hands and the new owner is in command. But in the case of special goods, such as extremely luxurious objects (for example, Louis Vuitton luggage or Jimmy Choo footwear), purposeful efforts are made by marketers in order to create and maintain among consumers a social commitment to specific rules of usage that will preserve and honour the image of the brand. Think for instance of the controversial marketing situations that arise when a luxury brand (for example, a producer of very fine French wine) seeks to prevent or even disqualify some heterodox usage of its products (drinking an expensive champagne 'on the rocks', for instance). One interesting example of this was the boycott that hip hop artist Jay-Z launched in 2006 against Louis Roederer's premium champagne, Cristal, after a representative of the French brand expressed discomfort about this champagne being popular among North American hip hop stars. (Cristal, renamed 'Crissy' by rappers, had even turned into an ingredient of hip hop luxury paraphernalia in songs and video clips). Heterodox usages are possible and marketing strategies may very well cope with them, but the fact that they may be felt to be controversial shows the extent to which a 'spirit of the commodity' (and the active presence of the 'name' of the producer) is a crucial ingredient of marketing.

Manufacturers, retailers and service providers often base their strategies on market research. This analyses consumers' attachments in order better to understand them (for a historical overview, see Tedlow, 1989). Market-research professionals use a wide array of investigative techniques. Some are quantitative, as in the case of the statistical examination of the purchasing behaviour of a set of consumer panels. Other techniques are qualitative, as is the case with focus groups. In a focus group, a small set of consumers (usually between six and eight) will be invited to discuss a particular activity – say, eating breakfast. A moderator will then try to channel the conversation towards a particular item such as cereals, and then towards particular brands and particular flavours with the intention of obtaining information about how consumers differentiate products and elaborate their preferences.

One particularly prevalent ingredient of attachment processes in commercial life is the individualisation or 'singularisation' of goods; that is, the establishment of a good's singularity and difference (Callon et al., 2002). In fact, tailoring and customising a good so as to make it adjust to a particular kind of consumer is central to many marketing activities.

This is apparent in the following discussion, by Lizabeth Cohen, of the evolution of haircare advertisements that appeared in a magazine targeting African-American readers in the USA (see Figure 4.4). As you read the extract, you should note the ways in which the singularisation of the product was a key element of the advertisers' evolving strategies for promoting consumer attachment to their clients' products.

Figure 4.4

The singularisation of products in advertising: since the 1950s, haircare advertising has become increasingly tailored to the needs of a black market

Reading 4.3   Lizabeth Cohen, 'A consumer's republic: the politics of mass consumption in postwar America

These three hair-care ads that appeared in *Ebony* magazine chart how mainstream manufacturers shifted their strategy of appealing to

This emphasis on mediating devices also draws attention to the *material* dimensions of social worlds. The perspective put forward in this chapter is not 'materialistic' in the sense of advocating a utilitarian, dehumanised view of economic life. Nor does it derive from a tradition of 'dialectical materialism' (i.e. Marxism), one that seeks to explain the evolution of economic life (including its ideological contents) as the complex result of the evolution of production forces and the accumulation of capital. Rather, the chapter can be said to adopt a 'material perspective' in the sense that it conceives of economic life as embedded in the material objects that circulate in exchange and in the technical devices that make such exchange possible.

With this in mind, we can now summarise the main arguments the chapter has explored. The example of music, dealt with in Section 2, suggests that there is no unique sociological perspective for the study of attachment. Among the possible alternatives, we can identify approaches attentive to the social factors that determine individual preferences, and those focusing more on the experience of attachment or the *means* by which attachment is actively achieved. From the point of view of cultural consumption, this example suggests the extent to which in economic life persons and things can become closely entangled.

Having established this framework, the chapter then addressed questions of economic exchange. In particular, in Section 3 it introduced the work of Mauss and other anthropologists interested in gift economies: the analysis of the process through which gifts and counter-gifts produce entanglement between persons. Examples taken from this anthropological literature, such as the Melanesian *kula*, exemplify how the circulation of gifts creates a network of mutually obliged persons.

Following on from this, the chapter explored in Section 4 how circulating objects are marked so as to make the giver present to the receiver. As the work of Zelizer demonstrates, apparently identical economic transfers can be understood as creating completely different social worlds depending on the extent to which the transfer is framed as an attachment or as a detachment.

The distinction between attachment and detachment was then further investigated in Section 5 which, in contrast to the emphasis on processes of attachment in gift exchange, explored the ways in which detachment operates as a key component of market exchange: a form of exchange that allows parties to be 'quits'. However, as Section 5 stressed, although detachment devices are an important aspect of market exchange, empirical market situations frequently combine several forms of attachment and detachment. Using examples from economic sociology, the section explored how a network of mutually obliged persons can sometimes prove of benefit in promoting fruitful business relations. This is captured in the concept of 'embeddedness': the extent to which market transactions are 'embedded' in social relations. Attention to the empirical variety of markets suggests that different market architectures can translate into different degrees of embeddedness with more or less beneficial consequences.

The chapter's penultimate section then took a closer look at the techniques and devices that are used in order to construct attachment and detachment in economic exchange. As the section showed, attachment and detachment are not spontaneous processes but are instead mediated by attachment and detachment techniques. Marketing and merchandising provide key examples of the former whereas clearing techniques provide equally significant illustrations of the latter. By focusing on such forms of mediation, Section 6 also drew attention to the fact that attachment and detachment are not purely subjective processes, but necessarily take forms that are material in nature.

By way of conclusion, you may want to reflect on the topic discussed in Section 2 – music – in the light of the arguments the chapter has subsequently developed. Music is, among other things, an economic object that circulates and changes hands, an object that is in fact at the centre of a whole industry. It is thus, or can be in some circumstances, a commodity. But it is a particular sort of commodity, one that is, to some extent, still bound to its author, whether understood as the composer or performer. How would you analyse the controversies over property rights in musical work that frequently occur? What can you say anthropologically of the attitude (shared by some consumers and musicians) that musical work should be considered a gift rather than a commodity? How would you understand the role of material objects, such as the CD leaflets accompanying musical works, in expressing the musician's presence? As you can perhaps see, music provides us with some intriguing questions through which to explore further the ideas presented in this chapter.

References

Bénatouïl, T. (1999) 'A tale of two sociologies: the critical and the pragmatic stance in contemporay French sociology', *European Journal of Social Theory*, vol. 2, no. 3, pp. 379–96.

Bourdieu, P. (1984) *Distinction: A Social Critique of the Judgement of Taste* (trans. R. Nice), London, Routledge and Kegan Paul.

Callon, M. (1998) 'Introduction: the embeddedness of economic markets in economics' in Callon (ed.) (1998).

Chapter 5
What does psychoanalysis contribute to our understanding of failures of social connectedness?

Michael Rustin

Contents

1   Introduction

This chapter explores the contribution which psychoanalytic thinking can make to our understanding of social connectedness or, more particularly, to those moments in which social connectedness fails. As the Introduction (see Section 1) to this volume argued, social worlds are made durable, in part, as a result of the processes of attachment and detachment 'by which people and objects are assembled into the regular, patterned and relatively stable arrangements that make up the social landscape'. In focusing on moments in which these processes come apart, the chapter will argue that there is a dimension of feelings in the lives of individuals, groups and societies which is often neglected by the social sciences, but is nevertheless powerful in its effects and fundamental to individual and social well-being. It will propose that psychoanalysis provides one of the most powerful resources for thinking about these sentient dimensions of social life, and that its concepts of 'unconscious mental processes' and the 'internal world' are fundamental for understanding how 'irrational forces' continually intervene to influence individual and social experience. The psychoanalytic idea of the dynamic unconscious also explains why this affective dimension of experience often goes unrecognised, and, in consequence, can be all the more disruptive and ungovernable in its effects.

In addressing these issues, the chapter is divided into eight sections. Section 2 opens by discussing the central role that questions of social connectedness have played in the development of sociology as a discipline and asks what psychoanalytic theory and practice can add to these debates. In answering this question, the section investigates the work of the founder of psychoanalysis, Sigmund Freud, and suggests that, although his major psychoanalytic ideas were developed initially to understand individual psychopathology, they nevertheless have relevance beyond the consulting room, helping us to understand issues of social connection and their failure in institutions, groups and in society at large.

These ideas are then developed in Section 3 through the work of the Austrian-born, British psychoanalyst, Melanie Klein. In particular, the section explores a famous study, conducted by Isabel Menzies Lyth (and extracted as Reading 5.1), of the effects of unconscious anxiety as this manifested itself in an institution engaged in training nurses (Menzies Lyth, 1988 [1959]). Unconscious anxiety is then explored, in Section 4, in relation to conflicts of 'race', ethnicity and religion and, in Section 5, in relation to the cold war. In particular, Section 5 discusses the arguments put forward by a leading post-Kleinian Polish-born psychoanalyst, Hanna Segal (1997 [1987]) in her article, 'Silence is the real crime' (extracted as Reading 5.2). The chapter then turns, in

Section 6, to an exploration of the work of another leading British psychoanalyst, Wilfred Bion. Bion's ideas – most especially, the notion of problems with 'thinking' – are applied, in the chapter's penultimate section, to the case of Victoria Climbié, an eight-year-old girl whose murder, in February 2000, led to widespread concern about child protection in England and Wales. In the chapter's final reading (Reading 5.3), the child psychotherapist Margaret Rustin (2005) reflects on the findings of the official inquiry into Victoria Climbié's death, arguing that this suggests the widespread presence, among child-protection personnel, of borderline states of mind. The chapter concludes by drawing these various arguments together, in particular with reference to their ability to illuminate questions related to 'mediation' and the relationship between the 'individual and the social': two of the sociological 'concerns' identified in the Introduction to this volume.

1.1 Teaching aims

The aims of this chapter are to:

- Introduce the particular contribution which psychoanalytic ideas about unconscious mental process can make to our understanding of moments in which social attachments and connectedness break down.

- Show that ideas drawn from different phases in the development of psychoanalysis in Britain illuminate these issues.

- Give examples of the ways in which unconscious states of mind give rise to social problems, or impede their solution by rational means.

- Explore the implications of these arguments for our understanding of 'mediation' and the relationship between the 'individual and the social.'

2 Social connectedness, sociology and the contribution of psychoanalysis

Explaining the preconditions for social connectedness and social order has been a central issue – perhaps *the* central issue – for sociology, and before it of political philosophy, since the beginnings of modern market societies in Europe in the seventeenth and eighteenth centuries. The question was, how were existing social worlds to hold together when the bonds of religion, tradition, community and kinship weakened as the modern world of individualism, greater mobility, market exchange, industrialisation and urbanisation came into being. Sociology as a field of study emerged in the nineteenth century in part as an attempt to answer this question. The classical sociologists – Durkheim, Weber,

Tönnies and Simmel, and their twentieth-century successors – tried to map the transition from 'traditional' to 'modern' societies as their major topic of investigation. Could institutions based on law and contract, they asked, take the place of religion, custom and hierarchical dependency as an adequate basis for social solidarity? This debate has continued into the twenty-first century, as contemporary theorists of 'globalisation' and 'individualisation' draw attention to what they perceive to be the further weakening of established social boundaries (see, for example, Bauman, 2000; Urry, 2000).

Psychoanalysis entered this debate early in the twentieth century, through the writings of Freud. The sources of integration and disintegration within individuals and societies were a central issue for Freud's new psychoanalytic field of study. As modern urban and industrial society emerged in the late nineteenth century, psychoanalysis drew attention to powerful irrational forces which liberal theories of progress had glossed over in their optimistic view of the universal advance of reason and science. In particular, the First World War, with its millions of dead, gave reason for Freud (1955a [1920]) to emphasise the strength of what he called the 'death instinct', a concept of powerful destructive impulses whose relevance seemed only to increase in the light of the violent struggles which characterised European political life between the two world wars.

Figure 5.1
Sigmund Freud

The main field of psychoanalytic practice has always been the clinical consulting room, and its primary interest was to understand and to alleviate, through its 'talking cure', the psychopathologies of individuals. Its approach differed from that of most social and medical science in giving great weight to the 'irrational' elements of the human psyche, the instincts and desires which Freud placed at the core of his theory of motivation. Freud believed that individuals were born with libidinal and aggressive drives which only became reconciled with the rules and restraints necessary for life in society with great difficulty. Freud's (1955b [1909]) theory of the Oedipus conflict describes the crucial early stage of a developmental struggle in which instinctual impulses in infants become repressed and inhibited. In an account found shocking because of its assertion of the reality of infantile sexuality, Freud described what he saw as the instinctual rivalry of the male infant for the love and possession of his mother. Through the 'repression' of infantile desires, and the development of a positive identification with the father-figure in place of rivalry with him, the infant learns to take his place in the social order (as Freud saw it) in which differences of gender and generation are accepted as natural and binding. (It is probably worth noting that Freud's apparent expectation that this process should, in 'normal' circumstances, have a specifically heterosexual outcome has been much criticised in recent years, and many psychoanalysts no longer think of sexuality in these terms.) A parallel pattern of development was said to take place for female infants, though perhaps less traumatically since the baby girl's intense attachments to her mother are not interrupted in the same way as the baby boy's. This is because, so it is claimed, girls are able to maintain their initial identification with their mothers, whereas boys must break this initial identification and make a new identification with their fathers.

Freud (1961a [1923]) also developed a tripartite model of the personality, in which the id is the site of unbridled desire, the ego describes the 'rational self' and the capacity to negotiate reality ('the reality principle'), while the superego represents internalised parental authority, prescribing what is right and wrong. In favourable developmental circumstances, the libidinal and destructive drives are later said to become 'sublimated' into the activities of creative work, art or science. 'Repression' – the process by which desires were rendered unconscious and therefore unthinkable – was, Freud argued, an unavoidable concomitant of normal development, but he held that the damage done by repression, through the action of the part of the mind he called the superego (what we ordinarily call the conscience), would be lessened if there could be a greater understanding and tolerance of psychic reality. If individuals could better recognise and understand their inner desires, and 'negotiate' some settlement with them, Freud suggested, they and society would do better than by denying that such desires exist.

Freud extended his thinking from the role of the unconscious mind within the individual psyche to its broader role in society and culture. Indeed, these dimensions were always connected in Freud's mind, since he recognised that the excessive repression of sexual and other desires from which his individual patients suffered was in part the effect on them of broader social prohibitions. In one of his contributions to our understanding of the role of the unconscious in society he described, for instance, how people could lose their sense of individual identity, and their powers of reason, if they became immersed in the passions of a group (Freud, 1961b [1930]). Freud held that the emotions and beliefs which originate in our attachment to our original parental objects become unconsciously projected into figures in our later experience. Freud recognised this phenomenon of 'transference' as it manifested itself in the consulting room, in the unconscious feelings (whether dependent, sexual or hostile) which patients directed towards their analyst, and this idea became crucial to the development of psychoanalytic practice (see Chapter 2 in this volume for ways in which this concept has been developed). But he also recognised that individuals, especially when their sense of identity was diminished by collectively shared emotions, projected feelings of infantile dependence, fear and admiration on a larger social plane, onto the leaders of groups and even whole societies. These unconscious projections gave rise to very unstable kinds of social order.

From the ideas Freud developed in his writings have developed many subsequent insights into the role of the unconscious in groups and society. The next section explores some of these later developments in psychoanalytic thinking, as a basis for showing how they can illuminate contemporary problems of social connection and disconnection.

3   The psychoanalytic idea of unconscious anxiety

One of the most important developments in psychoanalysis came from what has come to be called the 'object relations school', in part, associated with the work of Klein who significantly revised Freud's view of early development. For Freud (1957 [1914]), the starting point of infantile life was a state of 'primary narcissism', in which the baby recognised no existence other than its own. In contrast, Klein argued that infants were born in a state of innate psychological relatedness to others. (Later empirical research on infants and their capacity to differentiate the voice and smell of their mother from any other almost from birth has lent support to this claim – see, for example, Klaus and Kennell, 1976; Stern, 1985.)

Where, in Freud's theory of development, the problem was how the self's limitless desires could become reconciled with the needs of others, for Klein the primary issue was the infant's experience of its relations with its mother, and with the anxieties which inevitably arose within this relationship. Klein (1986 [1946]) described two psychological 'positions' which infants experienced. She saw these both as phases of development during the first months of life and as psychic structures which had a persistent existence throughout the lifespan. The first of these was the 'paranoid-schizoid position', and the second the 'depressive position', and each was defined by its characteristic form of anxiety. In the paranoid-schizoid position, anxiety is said to focus on imagined threats to the self, while in the depressive position, the dominant anxiety is said to focus on damage 'phantasied' to have been inflicted to the self's objects of attachment (the Kleinians signify their view of fantasy as an unconscious process by spelling it 'phantasy', differentiating it from the everyday use of fantasy as an activity of the imagination).

Klein described the psychic defences deployed by the self against these anxieties. One of the defences she identified was 'splitting', a process in which all good qualities are said to be attached to the self, and all bad qualities are felt to lie outside. Related to this is the idea of 'projection', discussed previously in Chapter 2 of this volume, in which aspects of the self are said to be projected into others, whom we then perceive in a distorted way, since unconsciously they now have our own attributes. (For example, we may accuse someone of shouting at us, when it is we who are shouting, not them.) The 'depressive' kind of anxiety, which arises from concern about damage suffered by others close to us, is said to be painful to bear in a different way, since it requires that we recognise our own responsibility for the harm that we have done, in reality or in phantasy, to our love-objects. Grief, loss and guilt are painful to experience, and reparation (the positive impulse to put right which we are said to experience in the depressive position) may not seem possible or sufficient. Thus, the dominant patterns of feeling described by Klein are the states of **unconscious anxiety** which arise in our most emotionally intense relationships with others, and are inseparable from them. (For a clear introduction to Klein's ideas, see Likierman, 2001.)

The severity of these anxieties and their consequences depends, Klein argued, on the balance of the libidinal and destructive instincts (the dispositions to love and hate) which prevails within the self. Although this balance in any individual may be in part a matter of innate disposition, it is also said to be greatly influenced by the quality of the infant's earliest nurturing relationships, and by how far these have allowed us to introject or internalise loved and loving 'internal objects' within the self (for a further discussion of internal objects, see Chapter 2, Section 3.1, in this volume).

Figure 5.2
Working with the sick and dying brings nurses into contact with the physical and mental pain of others

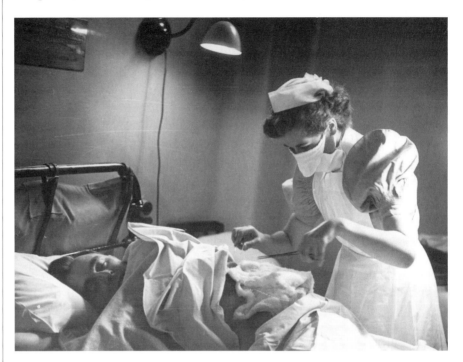

These ideas have had interesting applications to social as well as clinical situations. In particular, the idea of unconscious defences against anxiety has proved fruitful in understanding failings in institutions, especially those concerned with health and social care. This is important, since the failure of institutions to care adequately for those in their care can cause pain and damage to social bonds. A study by Menzies Lyth, 'The functioning of social systems as a defence against anxiety' (1988 [1959]) made a pioneering contribution to the understanding of unconscious anxieties in situations of this kind. She undertook this research as a consultant to a hospital which had become worried by the high levels of absence and sickness of nursing staff, and by the large number of trainee nurses who failed to finish their training or who left nursing soon after being trained. What was her explanation for these dysfunctions in the hospital nursing system?

Menzies Lyth observed that the nurses' work was organised in an exceptionally bureaucratic way, which required them to perform routine and unnecessary tasks 'by the book', and prevented them from exercising autonomy or initiative. She noticed that patients were referred to impersonally, for example, by the name of their illness and the number of their bed, rather than by their names. There seemed to be no commitment to nurses establishing a relationship with patients as individuals. Indeed, the whole nursing system seemed designed to prevent this from happening.

To explain this situation, Menzies Lyth suggested that what was being denied in the work of the hospital was the anxiety aroused in nurses, especially young and inexperienced ones, by their contact with the patients, their damaged bodies, and their physical and mental pain. Menzies Lyth saw the mindless routines of the ward as a form of defence against unconscious anxieties, as a way of suppressing and denying feelings. It was an unsuccessful defence, she suggested, since sickness and absence levels were high, and morale very low. She proposed that it would be better to provide space in which nurses could think and talk about their experiences, and encourage them to relate to their patients as people. A better quality of human contact between nurses and patients, and more understanding and supportive relationships between junior and senior nurses, would not remove the sources of these anxieties, which are inherent in hospital work, but would make them more bearable. A more personal style of nursing would also make it possible for nurses to experience and enjoy their patients' resilience and their appreciation of the work the nurses did for them. Menzies Lyth's and other related work has had a long-term influence in the health and social care fields with the result that, in recent years, the idea has gained ground that the emotional and relational dimensions of such work (sometimes called 'emotional labour') should be taken into account (Hochschild, 2003; Smith, 1992).

The following extract from Menzies Lyth's classic paper describes the nature and effects of unconscious anxiety within the hospital she studied. As you read it, try to identify the precise features of the nurse's experience that, according to Menzies Lyth, provoke unconscious anxiety.

Reading 5.1 Isabel Menzies Lyth, 'The functioning of social systems as a defence against anxiety'

Nature of the anxiety

The situations likely to evoke stress in nurses are familiar. Nurses are in constant contact with people who are physically ill or injured, often seriously. The recovery of patients is not certain and will not always be complete. Nursing patients who have incurable diseases is one of the nurse's most distressing tasks. Nurses are confronted with the threat and the reality of suffering and death as few lay people are. Their work involves carrying out tasks which, by ordinary standards, are distasteful, disgusting and frightening. Intimate physical contact with patients arouses strong libidinal and erotic wishes and impulses that may be difficult to control. The work situation arouses very strong and mixed feelings in the nurse: pity, compassion and love; guilt and anxiety; hatred and resentment of the patients who arouse these strong feelings; envy of the care given to the patient.

The objective situation confronting the nurse bears a striking resemblance to the phantasy situations that exist in every individual in the deepest and most primitive levels of the mind. The intensity and complexity of the nurse's anxieties are to be attributed primarily to the peculiar capacity of the objective features of her work situation to stimulate afresh these early situations and their accompanying emotions. I will comment briefly on the main relevant features of these phantasy situations.

The elements of these phantasies may be traced back to earliest infancy. The infant experiences two opposing sets of feelings and impulses, libidinal and aggressive. These stem from instinctual sources and are described by the constructs of the life instinct and the death instinct. The infant feels omnipotent and attributes dynamic reality to these feelings and impulses. He believes that the libidinal impulses are literally life-giving and the aggressive impulses death-dealing. The infant attributes similar feelings, impulses and powers to other people and to important parts of people. The objects and the instruments of the libidinal and aggressive impulses are felt to be the infant's own and other people's bodies and bodily products. Physical and psychic experiences are very intimately interwoven at this time. The infant's psychic experience of objective reality is greatly influenced by his own feelings and phantasies, moods and wishes.

Through his psychic experience the infant builds up an inner world peopled by himself and the objects of his feelings and impulses. In this inner world, they exist in a form and condition largely determined by his phantasies. Because of the operation of aggressive forces, the inner world contains many damaged, injured, or dead objects. The atmosphere is charged with death and destruction. This gives rise to great anxiety. The infant fears for the effect of aggressive forces on the people he loves and on himself. He grieves and mourns over their suffering and experiences depression and despair about his inadequate ability to put right their wrongs. He fears the demands that will be made on him for reparation and the punishment and revenge that may fall on him. He fears that his libidinal impulses and those of other people cannot control the aggressive impulses sufficiently to prevent utter chaos and destruction. The poignancy of the situation is increased because love and longing themselves are felt to be so close to aggression. Greed, frustration and envy so easily replace a loving relationship. This phantasy world is characterized by a violence and intensity of feeling quite foreign to the emotional life of the normal adult.

The direct impact on the nurse of physical illness is intensified by her task of meeting and dealing with psychological stress in other people ... .

Patients and relatives have very complicated feelings towards the hospital, which are expressed particularly and most directly to nurses, and often puzzle and distress them. Patients and relatives show appreciation, gratitude, affection, respect; a touching relief that the hospital copes; helpfulness and concern for nurses in their difficult task. But patients often resent their dependence; accept grudgingly the discipline imposed by treatment and hospital routine; envy nurses their health and skills; are demanding, possessive and jealous. Patients, like nurses, find strong libidinal and erotic feelings stimulated by nursing care, and sometimes behave in ways that increase the nurses' difficulties: for example by unnecessary physical exposure. Relatives may also be demanding and critical, the more so because they resent the feeling that hospitalization implies inadequacies in themselves. They envy nurses their skill and jealously resent the nurse's intimate contact with 'their' patient.

In a more subtle way, both patients and relatives make psychological demands on nurses which increase their experience of stress. The hospital is expected to do more than accept the ill patient, care for his physical needs, and help realistically with his psychological stress. The hospital is implicitly expected to accept and, by so doing, free patients and relatives from certain aspects of the emotional problems aroused by the patient and his illness. The hospital, particularly the nurses, must allow the projection into them of such feelings as depression and anxiety, fear of the patient and his illness, disgust at the illness and necessary nursing tasks. Patients and relatives treat the staff in such a way as to ensure that the nurses experience these feelings instead of – or partly instead of – themselves: for example by refusing or trying to refuse to participate in important decisions about the patient and so forcing responsibility and anxiety back on the hospital. Thus, to the nurses' own deep and intense anxieties are psychically added those of the other people concerned. As we became familiar with the work of the hospital, we were struck by the number of patients whose physical condition alone did not warrant hospitalization. In some cases, it was clear that they had been hospitalized because they and their relatives could not tolerate the stress of their being ill at home.

...

By the nature of her profession the nurse is at considerable risk of being flooded by intense and unmanageable anxiety. That factor alone, however, cannot account for the high level of anxiety so apparent in nurses. It becomes necessary to direct attention to the other facet of the problem – that is, to the techniques used in the nursing service to contain and modify anxiety.

Reading source
Menzies Lyth, 1988 [1959], pp. 46–50

As Menzies Lyth's argument suggests, from the point of view of this Kleinian version of psychoanalytic theory, objective features of the external world (in this instance, such things as intimate physical contact with suffering and damaged bodies) are liable to provoke early and very primitive forms of unconscious anxiety in those dealing with them. In an organisational context, Menzies Lyth suggests, unconscious anxiety may interrupt and damage not only relations between staff and the organisation's clients or customers, but also relations between staff and other staff (as was evidenced in the high absentee and drop-out rates on the nurse training course Menzies Lyth was studying). In effect, failure to recognise and deal with unconscious anxiety will result in what, following Jacques (1955), Menzies Lyth identifies as malign forms of 'socially structured defence mechanisms': organisational cultures and patterns of work that mirror primitive defence mechanisms, such as those characteristic of paranoid-schizoid states of mind (Menzies Lyth, 1988 [1959], p. 50).

A key example of this, identified by Menzies Lyth in a later passage in the same article, concerns relations between more senior and more junior members of nursing staff in the hospital (Menzies Lyth, 1988 [1959], pp. 56–7). These relations, Menzies Lyth argues, were characterised precisely by defensive splitting and projection, indicative of paranoid-schizoid states of mind. For instance, more senior nursing staff tended to describe junior staff as uniformly 'irresponsible' while junior staff tended to describe senior staff as uniformly 'severe'. Menzies Lyth explains these blanket characterisations as a defence against contradictory anxieties and desires. Caring for patients is, she argues, burdensome and presents nurses with many opportunities to behave in ways that are inappropriate (for example, aggressively). In short, nursing inevitably arouses the desire to be 'irresponsible'. Equally, as Menzies

Lyth goes on to explain, the heavy burden of responsibility nurses face arouses in them intensely self-critical responses. They will, for instance, chastise themselves for their irresponsible desires or perceived failures in care. In order to manage these contradictory feelings, Menzies Lyth suggests both senior and junior staff unconsciously projected what were in essence difficult or troubling aspects of themselves onto each other: junior staff became 'irresponsible'; senior staff 'punishing'. Her point is, of course, that this was not a purely individual process but something that had become structured into the ongoing day-to-day relations between these grades of staff. As this illustrates, Menzies Lyth's study suggests that unconscious anxiety, if not appropriately addressed, will interfere with an organisation's ability to develop productive mechanisms of attachment and detachment and thereby its ability to maintain the organisation as a relatively benign and durable social world.

4   Unconscious anxiety and conflicts of race and religion

Menzies Lyth's analysis of workplace cultures draws our attention to the significant role that unconscious anxieties can play within organisations. However, it is possible to argue that the psychoanalytic concepts such as persecutory and depressive anxiety are not only relevant to our understanding of social connectedness within organisations but can also illuminate wider aspects of social conflict – aspects which might otherwise escape our understanding, and be all the more difficult to resolve as a consequence.

One phenomenon to which the notion of unconscious anxiety seems particularly relevant is that of racism. There are, of course, many sources of racism, including the historical legacies of European and American slavery, the consequences of colonial rule, and the instrumental use of alleged differences of race in some societies to justify economic advantages and privileges. However, it is difficult to avoid the conclusion that there is something fundamentally irrational in the attributions of inferiority to peoples on grounds of race. It is this irrationality, this aspect of an unconsciously charged 'excess' of emotional investment in differences, to which psychoanalysis gives its particular attention (Rustin, 1991; Clarke, 2003).

It is now well established that there are virtually no significant genetic differences between human beings, except in superficial bodily attributes such as skin colour, facial configuration, and texture of hair (Lewontin, 1972). Yet races and ethnic groups are assigned a multiplicity of qualities to justify their treatment as inferiors. In the most extreme case of racialisation, that found in Nazi Germany, so-called inferior races such as

Jews were defined as sub-human, and deprived of all human entitlements, including life itself. While Nazism provides a particularly extreme example, the state of affairs in which members of other groups or communities are defined as innately inferior to one's own occurs frequently and widely. What is going on in the psychology of individuals and groups when this happens?

From a psychoanalytic point of view, it can be argued that ethnic or racial prejudice and stigmatisation is shaped in part by the unconscious mechanisms of 'splitting' and 'projection' described in the previous section. Groups may be hated or despised for attributes which have largely been projected onto them by their persecutors. The objects of such projections are then misperceived as possessing these negative qualities, and rejected or attacked because of them. For example, it can be argued that, in relation to the Northern Irish 'Troubles' of the last thirty years of the twentieth century, the Protestants hated the Catholics in part because the latter's supposedly more indulgent lifestyle (with its lesser respect for the work ethic and for bodily abstinence) aroused jealousy and envy for enjoyments which had to be renounced in a more repressive culture. This psychological dynamic, in which subordinate groups are disparaged for being less 'self-controlled' and 'rational' than those who dominate them, is a widespread one, and has been a potent legitimation of enslavement, colonial rule and paternalism. Subjugated groups are deemed to be too irrational or childish to be allowed freedom and autonomy.

A reverse projection can also take place, in which groups may be envied for the good qualities which they are deemed to have 'stolen' from their original possessors. In England, for example, it is possible to argue that post-war immigrants from the Indian subcontinent have aroused envy and resentment because they are seen to uphold virtues of extended family solidarity and support which were earlier a source of pride in the English industrial working class, but which have been undermined by economic decline. In other words, not only do members of the indigenous community feel they have been 'robbed' of housing and jobs, but also of a social identity that is felt to have been damaged.

Such projections of feeling into a group which is powerless to resist them can also have damaging effects on those 'projected into'. Real psychic injury may be caused if one is made to suffer persistent disrespect and disregard. As is suggested by the figure of 'Uncle Tom' in the history of African Americans in the USA, psychological defence may even be sought by conforming to a projected definition, since at least some relationship can then be established with the powerful, even if on disadvantageous terms. The situation may be experienced as one in which *any* recognised identity is better than being allowed none at all.

The greater the levels of anxiety in a community, brought about by its difficulty in sustaining its solidarity and shared values, the more likely it is that hostility and resentment will be mobilised against alien groups who can be blamed for these misfortunes. For example, it can be argued that the defeat of Germany in the First World War, and the collapse of its economy after the Great Crash of 1929, played a major part in the mobilisation of racial hatred by the Nazis – an extreme form of splitting in which, as previously noted, all strength and goodness was attributed to a largely mythical Aryan race, and all weakness and evil to Jews, Slavs and other racial groups.

If racism, and ethnic and religious conflict offer potent examples in which processes of psychic splitting and projection seem to operate at the level of social groups and across wider social formations, we can also identify instances in which unconscious anxiety – although present – has been, to some degree, ameliorated. A compelling example of the latter is to be found in the sense of relief and hope which was evoked when Nelson Mandela was freed from imprisonment in 1990 and was later elected President of South Africa. From a psychoanalytic point of view, it is arguable that Mandela's exceptional lack of bitterness and vengefulness for the injustice and suffering to which he – like other members of the black and coloured populations – had been subjected, gave reassurance that, for once, a terrible cycle of violence and hatred might be broken. In effect, white South Africans were enabled to feel that they might avoid a punishment that, in phantasy, they must have felt they deserved. In particular, the Truth and Reconciliation Commission chaired by Desmond Tutu, then Archbishop of Cape Town and the leader of the Anglican Church's opposition to the apartheid regime, provided post-apartheid South Africa with a symbolic space in which wrongs could be acknowledged and where mourning could take place. The idea behind the Truth and Reconciliation Commission was that such a public process might mitigate if not resolve deep grievances and hatreds. However, many broader injustices – including that of apartheid itself – were deemed to be beyond the scope of this process, and the fact that, nearly two decades after Mandela's release, the country still experiences very high levels of violence, indicates how difficult it is to overcome such a legacy of injustice and to rebuild benign forms of social attachment and connectedness.

As this suggests, the history of apartheid in South Africa and the subsequent, post-apartheid attempts to address the legacy of this history provide powerful examples both of the role that unconscious anxiety can play in undermining benign forms of social connectedness and of the possible ways in which such anxieties can be – in however limited a fashion – ameliorated. Nonetheless, this example also points to the paradoxical nature of the relations of attachment and detachment that

Figure 5.3
Archbishop Desmond
Tutu hands President
Nelson Mandela a copy
of the report of the
Truth and
Reconciliation
Commission

unconscious anxiety can be said to promote. The group engaged in paranoid-schizoid splitting and projection is, of course, launching what is effectively an emotional (and sometimes physical) attack on the group that is the object of loathing. As such, the former group can be said to be detaching itself from the latter and is certainly undermining the possibility of benign forms of social connecting. Paradoxically, however, the group engaged in paranoid-schizoid splitting is, via projection, also emotionally entangled with and thereby attached to the group that is the object of loathing. In other words, from a psychoanalytic point of view, acts of detachment are, when fuelled by paranoid-schizoid states of mind, simultaneously acts of attachment that reveal profound confusion between self and other and between what is inside and what outside.

5 The cold war and the 'war on terror'

The discussion in the previous section indicated, in general terms, how the notion of unconscious anxiety can be applied to moments in which social connectedness fails. We can explore these arguments in more detail by turning to an extract from a famous article, 'Silence is the real crime', written by the psychoanalyst Segal (1997 [1987]). Originally published while the cold war was still in progress, the article argued that the cold war could be understood in part as a psychic structure shaped by paranoid-schizoid anxiety. The two sides – the former Soviet Union and the West – confronted one another with nuclear forces kept sometimes on hair-trigger alert and capable, if used, of destroying virtually all of modern society. Each side rationalised its stance as defensive and peaceful, even though throughout the cold war they waged many 'proxy' or peripheral wars in the developing world. Each camp was, after all, as prepared as the other to set off a nuclear Armageddon if it were attacked. Segal argued that these positions simultaneously enacted and denied powerful destructive impulses – the death instinct – each side ascribing these intentions wholly to its enemy, while professing its own peacefulness.

Figure 5.4

Boeing B-52 Stratofortress: During the cold war, B-52s were a significant component of the US nuclear deterrent. At least some carried the Strategic Air Command's motto, 'Peace is our profession'

Reading 5.2 is an extract from Segal's article, 'Silence is the real crime', setting out her view of the way in which unconscious anxieties sustained the system of nuclear deterrence. As you read the article, you may want to reflect on what exactly it is that, in Segal's view, reveals the presence of paranoid-schizoid states of mind within the military strategies of the opposing camps.

Reading 5.2   Hanna Segal, 'Silence is the real crime'

When we look soberly ... at the political situation and the threat of nuclear warfare, we observe a phenomenon that is more like a surrealist scenario, an unbearable nightmare or a psychosis, than a sane world. The Hiroshima bomb killed at one go 140,000 people and that does not include the many thousands who died from the after-effects or the zombie-like existence of the survivors ...

The nuclear arsenal of either Russia or America is enough to blow up the world many times over. And still they both continue to develop and stockpile nuclear weapons and contend that this is needed for security. The foreseeable effects of what is genteelly known as 'nuclear exchange' between Russia and America are well studied and documented by scientists. The medical evidence is that there will be no meaningful survival. There is growing scientific evidence that the exploding of only part of that arsenal will bring about a nuclear winter which will engulf all the northern hemisphere, if not the whole planet. These facts are constantly put before the public. Nevertheless, the urgency of the threat to human survival does not seem to have led to a concerted effort to stop what is happening. Indeed, the way things are going, it seems likely that a nuclear war may be an inevitable consequence.

Many take the view, especially in governmental circles, that the threat to the human race posed by nuclear weapons is minimized by mutual deterrence that is maintained by remaining vigilant, well-armed and technologically active. In a world of changing technology, this means constant research and upgrading of weapons and more and more powerful and destructive systems: the nuclear arms race. ... I believe, contrary to the prevailing governmental view, that the arms race and the theory of deterrence that supports and justifies it is actually dangerous. Psychoanalytic understanding can help us to see that the theory of deterrence and its current practice may actually lead to our destruction. It is this argument I want to develop and explain in this paper as part of a plea to psychoanalysts urgently to participate in active efforts to halt what I consider a mad process.

...

The idea of deterrence is to be stronger so as to frighten the enemy – to deter him from aggression. As the 1950 US National Security Document NSC 68 states: 'The only deterrent we can present to the Kremlin is evidence we give that we may make any of the critical points in the world which we cannot hold the occasion for a global war of annihilation.' But the enemy's reasoning is likely to be the same. Hence, the doctrine inevitably leads to escalating anxiety and to the arms race. The nuclear arms race is the heir to the nuclear deterrence. The 'defensive' preparations to counter aggression in which both sides in an arms race engage must create unstable fear. ... Preparing for war on both sides promotes the likelihood of a pre-emptive strike out of fear, and the equilibrium of a system of mutual deterrence is inherently unstable. Hatred leads to fear and fear to hatred in an ever-increasing vicious circle. ...

Psychoanalysis is very familiar with vicious circles of hatred and fear. It teaches us that in an individual, destructive and self-destructive drives can only be modified when the individual can get some insight into their motives and visualize the consequences to others and to themselves of their action. But we know that powerful defences operate against such insights. I suggest that there is some evidence that such resistances to knowing are active in our public life. For instance – there is a reluctance to visualize actual consequences of a nuclear war. We hear now that the use of nuclear weapons can be strategic or minimal. At the same time, there is some evidence that the governments do not clearly visualize the consequences of nuclear war. The civil defence plans, at least in Britain, are a case in point. When the British Medical Association was asked by the government to prepare a report on civil defence, the report said that there could be no meaningful preparation, since after a nuclear blast, there would be no communications, probably no doctors or nurses and no edible food. The British Government's response was to try to suppress this report. ... So governments both envisage a nuclear war and deny the reality of what it would entail.

This attitude involves the operation of denial. Close to denial, but not identical to it, is the turning of a blind eye. I think the mechanism here is of a particular form of splitting (described by Freud as disavowal, operating in perversions). In this split we retain intellectual knowledge of the reality, but divest it of emotional meaning. An example in public life is the fact that various opinion polls have revealed that the vast majority of people think that nuclear war is inevitable, and that probably there will be no survival. And yet the same vast majority live their lives in that shadow without taking active steps to change policy.

We wish to deny the consequences of our actions to others and to ourselves, and to deny any aggressive impulses or actions on our own part. Increases in armaments are often kept secret. Here the British Cabinet papers of the 1950s are again revealing. When Attlee started manufacturing the A-bomb it was in secret, not only from Parliament, but even from members of his own Cabinet. Similarly, when the Churchill Government undertook the manufacturing of the H-bomb, they avoided the substantial opposition they anticipated. The Cabinet Committee responsible disguised the extent of the atomic programme by hiding the cost under 'other current expenditure' and 'extra-mural research'. ... The hallowed word is 'security', but the secrecy, as those Cabinet notes make clear, is hardly motivated by having to hide from the enemy. Sooner or later the powers know all about one another's research. A note prepared for the Cabinet Committee said that the publicity could damage the West's defence interests, not because the Russians might learn something new, but because of the effect on public opinion. In dictatorial regimes like the USSR, this secrecy is built into the regime.

When our own aggressiveness can be disguised and hidden from us 'for security reasons', projective mechanisms and subsequent paranoia are increased. The enemy is presented as the devil. Mrs Thatcher speaks of the Russians as our hereditary enemy, yet since the Crimean War in 1854 the Russians have been Britain's allies in two world wars. President Reagan speaks of the Russians as the 'evil empire'.

...

This kind of functioning has been described in the individual as a regression from the depressive position, characterized by a capacity to recognize one's own aggression, and to experience guilt and mourning, and a capacity both to function in reality and to make reparation. The regression is to the paranoid-schizoid position, characterized by the operation of denial, splitting and projection. I am speaking here of mechanisms familiar in the individual (Klein, 1946, 1948). It could be argued that we cannot transfer such knowledge directly to behaviour of large groups. Nevertheless, such mechanisms can be seen in group behaviour. Fornari (1975) has described wars as a paranoid defence against depressive anxiety. Indeed, in groups such mechanisms may be increased.

References

Fornari, F. (1975) Psychoanalysis of Nuclear War, *Bloomington, IN, University of Indiana Press.*

Klein, M. (1946) 'Notes on some schizoid mechanisms', International Journal of Psycho-Analysis, *27, pp. 99–110; reprinted in* The Writings of Melanie Klein, *London,* The Hogarth Press, *3, pp. 1–24 (1975).*

Klein, M. (1948) 'On the theory of anxiety and guilt', International Journal of Psycho-Analysis, *28; reprinted in* The Writings of Melanie Klein, *London,* The Hogarth Press, *3, pp. 25–42 (1975).*

Reading source

Segal, 1997 [1987], pp. 143–7

In a subsequent article, Segal (1995) perceptively suggested that the end of the cold war (following the fall of the Berlin Wall in 1989) had resulted in the loss of the existing means of containment of these paranoid-schizoid impulses and would, in consequence, produce a crisis within social systems which had for decades been psychically organised by them. She argued that a new enemy would need to be found, or created, which would enable these 'structures of feeling' to be maintained without much modification. In Segal's view, the 1991 Gulf War against Iraq, launched in response to Saddam Hussein's invasion of Kuwait, served this psychic purpose, and was even perhaps permitted to take place because of this.

Needless to say, the events of '9/11' – the flight of manned civil aircraft into the Twin Towers of the World Trade Center in New York and the Pentagon in Washington, DC – can be thought of as greatly amplifying this dynamic, not least because of the highly symbolic nature of the damage they inflicted on the USA. In this light, the subsequent 'war on terror', including the US invasion of Afghanistan to destroy the Taliban and its support for al-Qaeda, and the invasion of Iraq in 2003, can be understood as reprisals that were motivated as much by psychic as by objective military factors. As Segal (1995) presciently suggested, the effect of all this has arguably been to construct a collective enemy of Islamic terrorism, one perceived by governments and public alike as a deadly threat to global safety. The irrational dimensions of this can surely be gauged by the fact the actual military power of Islamic terrorism seems small compared with that of the USA and its allies and is, in objective terms, much less of a threat than the danger posed to global security when the huge nuclear forces of the two cold war camps confronted one another.

As this suggests, the contribution of psychoanalysis to the understanding of conflicts – whether at local or international levels – is its attention to the distortions of reality, and to the excesses of passions and hatreds, which accompany them. From a psychoanalytic perspective, unconscious anxiety leads to an intolerance of complex realities, to a preference for certainty over uncertainty, and to a need to feel protected against enemies by membership of a group which feels homogeneous and strong.

6   Borderline states of mind

As you saw in Reading 5.2, as well as discussing the cold war in terms of paranoid-schizoid anxieties, Segal refers to a mental state that she calls 'turning a blind eye'. This reference points to a further evolution of psychoanalytic ideas, one associated most closely with the work of Bion (1963, 1967). Bion became interested through his work with psychotic patients in the preconditions for the development of the capacity for thinking. He proposed that the infantile anxiety theorised by Klein was in favourable conditions 'contained' by a relationship with a mother or equivalent carer, and that such containment essentially included the active mental function of processing feelings and thoughts beyond the capacity of an infant to cope with alone. Psychotic states, he suggested, might be the consequence of a failure of such a 'mental apparatus' to develop properly in early life. Bion's ideas have led to great attention being given to the 'containing' capacity of early relationships, and to the consequences of their weakness or absence. Symbolic or 'thinking capacity' (which refers particularly to the capacity to acknowledge and process emotions) becomes in this framework a defining aspect of mental health, relevant not only to the relations between parents and children, but also to relations between those taking many other caring roles – for example, teachers, doctors, nurses and some managers – and those for whom they have responsibility. Giving attention to this dimension of reflectiveness and symbolisation enhances understanding of what is missing when caring institutions fail to manage their particular task-related anxieties, or when members of groups and networks cease to be able to communicate thoughtfully with one another.

A related theoretical development in psychoanalysis was the understanding of a further psychic defence which was sometimes mobilised to escape the pain of paranoid-schizoid and depressive anxiety. This was the idea of narcissism, also described as a **'borderline' state of mind** (Spillius, 1988; Steiner, 1993). This concept signifies a retreat from the pain of an intense relationship with another, into a willed self-sufficiency, in which it is claimed that the self needs no one to sustain it, and in which others are often misrepresented as being too deficient to provide anything good even if it *were* needed. (This version of the concept of narcissism sees it as a defence against the pain of relationships with others, not as a primary condition of infantile mental life as Freud first held it to be.)

These ideas first arose in the treatment of psychoanalytic patients, whose refusal of a relationship with, or the understanding offered by, their therapist mirrored their personal situation outside the consulting room. The difficulty of establishing a relationship in feeling with such patients gave psychoanalysts a compelling clinical reason for learning to understand this kind of defence, since its effects made progress within the consulting room very difficult. However, the idea of a narcissistic or borderline defence has become applied more widely, in particular to the difficulties of institutions and social networks in responding to emotional pain. It has come to be realised that a state of 'not thinking', or virtual mindlessness, can afflict organisations and their members, destroying their capacity to work effectively – an issue investigated in the chapter's next section.

7 Failures in the child-protection system

Psychoanalytic thinking making use of the notion of borderline states of mind has been usefully brought to bear to understand a widely-publicised failure in the child-protection system in England and Wales, the case of Victoria Climbié. Victoria Climbié was a child aged eight who died while in the foster care of her aunt Kouao and her partner, having been abused by them with great cruelty for several months beforehand. This case was fully investigated by a Committee of Inquiry headed by Lord Laming, whose Report (DoH and HO, 2003) provided a very detailed account of the circumstances which had led up to this child's death.

The reason for the great public concern aroused by the case, aside from the tragedy of a child having died in these circumstances, was that the child and her carers were well known to several different elements of the childcare system, including social services, the National Health Service (NHS) and the police. Most distressingly of all, there was medical evidence of the child having been physically injured which was not followed up. A scheduled visit to investigate the child in her home was, for instance, cancelled because the social workers and police concerned had heard a rumour that there was an infection of scabies in the house which the professional visitors saw as an unacceptable risk to their own health. It seems that the facts of serious abuse of this child being committed over a considerable period were known in one way or another to many members of the network of services responsible for child protection, yet nothing effective was done.

Nor was this an isolated case. The effectiveness of services responsible for the care of children in Britain had on many previous occasions been

Figure 5.5

Francis and Berthe Climbié hold a copy of the Laming Inquiry report into the death of their daughter, Victoria

brought into question by disastrous failures to protect children in need. Cases which had led to the death of an individual child, included, among others, those of Maria Colwell (1973), Jasmine Beckford (1984), Tyra Henry (1984), and Kimberley Carlile (1986). Such cases had on several occasions been investigated by official inquiries, whose published reports had then become central documents in public discussion and in government decision making. Since these inquiries had invariably found that poor or negligent professional practice was in part responsible for the fate of the children concerned, they had led to a great deal of public criticism of the relevant services, and particularly of the social work profession.

What are the reasons for these endemic failures of professional practice, and what might be done to prevent their occurrence? These are obviously crucial questions for those responsible for or working in these services. Often the explanations given in successive inquiry reports have concerned specific errors of omission or commission, inadequacies in the laid-down procedures or a failure to follow them. The Victoria Climbié Report was no exception, concluding, as it did, with 108 recommendations whose purpose was to prevent such failures in future. Organisational reform, better inter-agency working, and clearer and stricter guidelines for the management of such situations were among them.

No doubt many of these recommendations were in themselves appropriate and sensible. Yet some have argued that this procedurally-driven approach fails to recognise a crucial aspect of the problem. From this point of view, the problem is not so much lack of appropriate procedures, but that those working in these systems often seem unable to follow procedures that already exist, or to act responsibly upon the facts that are available to them.

In a published discussion of the Climbié Inquiry Report, the child psychotherapist, Margaret Rustin has sought to understand the experiences and states of mind of those involved in the case, as the careful descriptions given in the Report made it possible to do. She suggests that a number of unrecognised and unconscious states of anxiety had inhibited the many preventive actions that could and should have been taken as the events of the case unfolded over many months.

These issues are explored in the following extract from Rustin's article. As you read it, you may find it helpful to reflect, in particular, on the specific ways in which, as Rustin sees it, narcissistic or borderline states of mind had come to dominate the working practices of those involved in caring for Victoria Climbié.

Reading 5.3   Margaret Rustin, 'Conceptual analysis of critical moments in Victoria Climbié's life'

Introduction

In this paper I draw on a number of concepts I have found useful in reading the important and deeply disturbing report into the death of Victoria Climbié produced by Lord Laming (The Stationery Office 2003). ... Some of the concepts I make use of are very close to everyday ideas. Others are drawn from psychoanalytic theory because I believe it illuminates the puzzling and repetitive facts revealed by the Inquiry. I shall pay particular attention to issues of mental pain, borderline functioning, infantile persecutory anxieties, confusion, defensive splitting and mirroring processes. The inadequate responses of individuals and institutions are, I argue, profoundly linked to the disturbing impact of what they are trying to manage. ...

Avoiding mental pain in child protection work

It seems essential to begin by paying attention to the central importance of the *mental* pain which all the individuals referred to by Lord Laming faced in their lives and work. Much of my commentary concerns the ways in which ordinary professionals doing difficult work may deploy defences against mental pain.

It is notable that while much emphasis is given in the Inquiry Report to the appalling nature of Victoria's physical injuries, there is little description of the mental agony she must have endured. No photographs can document that, of course, but I suspect that understanding the way in which mental pain is faced or avoided is crucial to making sense of the defensive evasion by large numbers of professionals which the report details.

What is it that, at root, is being avoided? I think a significant component is the psychological impact of becoming aware of Victoria's dreadful life circumstances. Defences against such awareness are much to the fore in the story reported, and defences against recognizing reality necessarily involve severe distortions in the mind's capacity to function. Of particular relevance are frequent examples of 'turning a blind eye' (Steiner 1985), that is, failing to see what is before one's eyes because to do so would cause too much psychic disturbance, and various forms of 'attacks on linking' (Bion 1967), the systematic disconnection between things which logically belong together, again a defence which is employed because to make the link would be a source of painful anxiety.

In psychoanalytic theory, these two forms of defence are frequently found to predominate in individuals with what is known as borderline pathology, and this fact alerts us to the massive level of dysfunction which Lord Laming's report depicts in social services, the health service and the police with respect to child protection work. He is clearly delineating organizations which might be described as functioning in a way analogous to the borderline patient (M.J. Rustin *et al.* 2003), organizations many of whose staff, at all levels of seniority, are unable to face reality and operate as a consequence in ways designed to protect them from the catastrophic impact that they believe a proper confrontation with reality would engender.

Psychoanalysts have described this form of defensive organization in individuals in various ways, but one of the most useful conceptualizations has been by John Steiner. He named the protective structures created by the individual who is dominated by fear of reality as 'psychic retreats' (Steiner 1993). Just as the individual patient can persuade himself unconsciously that reality can truly be avoided if he stays put within the narrow confines of his personal psychic retreat, so workers within the organizations described, and the organizations themselves as represented by their structures and practices, seem to have been convinced that they could escape having to think about their contact with Victoria and her aunt, Kouao. Thinking involves the attribution of meaning to our experience. Without a sense of meaning, it is difficult to imagine what personal responsibility for actions would amount to, and it is just this phenomenon which the report continually highlights.

The nature of the mental pain associated with borderline defences is specific: it concerns conflict between opposing forces, ultimately the forces of love and hate, and the guilt aroused by awareness of ambivalence. I think it is helpful to bear in mind that many of the actions (or moments of inaction) described in the report as obvious evidence of incompetence relate to the desire of professionals to keep a distance from the intense feelings stirred up by exposure to human cruelty and madness. The fear and hatred people felt is only occasionally hinted at.

Another disturbing and shocking theme is the level of dishonesty among witnesses. The everyday gloss on this is likely to attribute to the liar a conscious desire to escape blame. That is part of the story. It seems clear that evidence had been removed from various files with an explicit intention to deceive, and Lord Laming implies that some senior managers who changed their jobs after the tragedy may have been up to something equivalent. But the concept which may help us to understand more about what happened at the front line is that of unconscious mirroring between clients and professionals. Kouao's statements to the people who tried to help were full of both confusion and lies. It is often not at all simple to tell the difference between malicious dishonesty and the kind of confusion about truth which is part of borderline psychotic states. Kouao's behaviour during her later trial strongly suggests that her mental state was severely disturbed during this period; a serious personality disorder would be the probable diagnosis. The evidence of the report is that the impact of her confusion and distortion of the truth seems to have invaded the minds of many of those who came in contact with her, particularly once there was a relationship in which she was trying to get the other person to see things as she saw them. It is remarkable to see just how successful she was in this aim: doctors, social workers, police, clergymen and others were frequently acting on the belief that Victoria had something wrong with her. This was variously identified as a disease (scabies), behaviour problems (enuresis and other disturbed behaviour) and possession by an evil spirit, but in all instances the problem was agreed to be that Victoria needed to be cured, and the bad thing inside her got rid of. Such was Kouao's conviction, and the power of her vision continuously obscured the facts. I believe that processes of projective identification, in which the thinking of the professionals was taken over by elements of Kouao's madness, go some way to explain how this can have happened. Instead of being able to observe and thus question Kouao's belief system, workers began to mirror it (Britton 1981) ... .

Finally, the report causes one to ponder on the infantile anxieties which the tasks of child protection evoke in staff. Feelings of helplessness, of dependence and deference to authorities, of not knowing enough, of sticking to rules mindlessly like a terrorized child (indeed like Victoria herself in her observed behaviour in Kouao's presence), of fear and of wanting to return to the 'normal' world as soon as possible predominate. The kind of training and support made available to staff does not seem to have helped them to mobilize more adult mental capacities to cope with the unavoidable emotional disturbance of this difficult work.

References

Bion, W.R. (1967) 'Attacks on linking'. In Second Thoughts, pp. 110–119. Heinemann, London.

Britton R. (1981) 'Re-enactment as an unwitting professional response to family dynamics'. In: Psychotherapy with Families: An Analytic Approach (eds S. Box, B. Copley, J. Magagna and E. Moustaki), pp. 48–58. Routledge, London.

Rustin, M.J., Rustin, M.E., Anderson, J., Cohn, N., Hindle, D., Ironside, L. and Philps, J. (2003) Borderline Organizations. Paper given at conference of Tavistock Society of Psychotherapists.

Steiner, J. (1985) 'Turning a blind eye: the cover up for Oedipus'. International Review of Psychoanalysis, vol. 12, pp. 161–172.

Steiner, J. (1993) Psychic Retreats, Routledge, London.

The Stationery Office (2003) The Victoria Climbié Inquiry Report. The Stationery Office, London.

Reading source

Rustin, 2005, pp. 11–13

As Rustin makes clear, those charged with the care of Victoria Climbié seemed to have found it very difficult to 'think'. Realities were denied and responsibility was passed around. Everyone waited for someone else to act, while no one did what was necessary until it was too late. Rustin suggests that this situation is not an uncommon one in the services responsible for childcare, even though, in this instance, its outcome was an exceptional tragedy. Accounting for this phenomenon, Rustin describes a kind of 'mindlessness', or in psychoanalytic terms a 'borderline state', which can set in within systems overburdened by a large number of cases in which children are in great need. The idea of 'mindlessness' refers to a state of mind in which unconscious anxieties are defended against by not thinking, not feeling, or not seeing.

It follows, from this perspective, that such anxieties cannot be managed solely through instituting better rules and procedures (necessary as these may be). Anxieties need to be consciously acknowledged and worked through by all those concerned in a case, through appropriate kinds of report and discussion. Attention needs to be given to the training of staff, and the organisational and supervisory support given to them, if the mental pain inherent in this work is to be 'contained'. Only where this is done is it likely that work of good quality will be possible.

8   Conclusion

Like the other examples explored in this chapter, the failures in child protection that led to Victoria Climbié's death suggest that unconscious anxiety and the states of mind to which it gives rise can play a significant role in those moments in which social attachments and connectedness break down. The chapter has sought to argue that psychoanalytic ideas provide insights into these moments that are not available within other conceptual frames and that, in consequence, psychoanalytic ideas are a valuable addition to the sociological study of attachment and detachment processes. From this point of view, our ability to explain why benign processes of attachment and detachment do not always arise or persist – why social worlds are sometimes chaotic, violent and lacking in connection – depends on an understanding of the irrational and frequently unconscious dimensions of social life.

What, then, do these arguments tell us about mediation and the relationship between the individual and the social, two of the sociological 'concerns' identified in the Introduction to this book? As Chapter 2 in this volume has previously argued, one of the main contentions of psychoanalytic ideas is that our experience of social worlds is always *mediated* by the unconscious. The account of unconscious anxiety put forward in this chapter is clearly in this vein.

The social workers and other professionals discussed in Reading 5.3, like the nursing staff discussed by Menzies Lyth in Reading 5.1, were not, in any straightforward sense, wilfully negligent or bad at their jobs. Rather, their ability to act effectively was mediated, in fact compromised, by the unconscious anxiety that the distressing nature of their work aroused and by failures, at an organisational level, to address this anxiety in appropriate ways. Equally, the breakdown of social connections that characterised, for example, the apartheid state in South Africa or relations between the superpowers during the cold war, can be said to have been mediated by paranoid-schizoid states of mind.

As Chapter 2 also suggested, psychoanalytic arguments, although viewing the individual as endowed with inherent capacities and attributes – such as those of phantasy, splitting and projection – nevertheless tend to see individuals and the social worlds in which they live as being inextricably intertwined. Indeed, one of the key arguments this chapter has sought to develop is that states of mind usually associated with individuals (for example, those associated with paranoid-schizoid and borderline states) can also come to characterise the ways in which the members of an organisation or social group routinely relate to each other and to those with whom they come in contact. As Reading 5.1 illustrated, the existing practices of an organisation or social group can provoke or exacerbate these states of mind and, once entrenched, the states of mind can themselves mould practice, further provoking rather than ameliorating unconscious anxiety. In such circumstances, individuals and the social worlds in which they are located become entangled in mutually constitutive relations. The unconscious anxiety felt by an individual will be inextricably bound up – indeed, provoked and exacerbated by – the social world he or she inhabits even as that social world is, in part, actively shaped and remade by this unconscious anxiety and the defensive responses it promotes.

References

Bauman, Z. (2000) *Liquid Modernity*, Cambridge, Polity Press.

Bion, W. (1963) *Learning from Experience*, London, Heinemann.

Bion, W. (1967) *Second Thoughts*, London, Heinemann.

Clarke, S. (2003) *Social Theory, Psychoanalysis and Racism*, Basingstoke, Palgrave Macmillan.

Department of Health (DoH) and Home Office (HO) (2003) *The Victoria Climbié Inquiry*, London, The Stationery Office (Laming Report).

Freud, S. (1955a [1920]) 'Beyond the pleasure principle' in Strachey, J. (ed.) (1953–1966) *Standard Edition*, vol. 18.

Freud, S. (1955b [1909]) 'Analysis of a phobia in a five-year old child (The case of "Little Hans")' in Strachey (ed.) (1953–1966) *Standard Edition*, vol. 10.

Freud, S. (1957 [1914]) 'On narcissism: an introduction' in Strachey (ed.) (1953–1966) *Standard Edition*, vol. 14.

Freud, S. (1961a [1923]) 'The ego and the id' in Strachey (ed.) (1953–1966) *Standard Edition*, vol. 19.

Freud, S. (1961b [1930]) 'Civilisation and its discontents' in Strachey (ed.) (1953–1966) *Standard Edition*, vol. 21.

Hochschild, A.R. (2003) *The Managed Heart: The Commercialization of Human Feeling* (2nd edn), Berkeley, CA, University of California Press.

Jacques, E. (1955) 'Social systems as a defence against persecutory and depressive anxiety' in Klein, M., Heimann, P. and Money-Kyrle, R.E. (eds) *New Directions in Psycho-Analysis*, New York, NY, Basic Books.

Klaus, M. and Kennell J. (1976) *Maternal-Infant Bonding*, St Louis, MO, Mosby.

Klein, M. (1986 [1946]) 'Notes on some schizoid-mechanisms' in Mitchell, J. (ed.) *The Selected Melanie Klein*, Harmondsworth, Penguin/Peregrine.

Lewontin, R.C. (1972) 'The apportionment of human diversity', *Evolutionary Biology*, vol. 6, pp. 381–98.

Likierman, M. (2001) *Melanie Klein: Her Work in Context*, London, Continuum.

Menzies Lyth, I. (1988 [1959]) 'The functioning of social systems as a defence against anxiety: a report on a study of the nursing service of a general hospital' in Menzies Lyth, I. *Containing Anxiety in Institutions: Selected Essays, Volume 1*, London, Free Association Books.

Rustin, M. (2005) 'Conceptual analysis of critical moments in Victoria Climbié's life', *Child and Family Social Work*, vol. 10, no. 1, pp. 11–19.

Rustin, M.J. (1991) 'Psychoanalysis, racism and anti-racism' in Rustin, M.J. *The Good Society and the Inner World*, London, Verso.

Segal, H. (1995) 'From Hiroshima to the Gulf War and after: a psychoanalytic perspective' in Elliott, A. and Frosh, S. (eds) *Psychoanalysis in Contexts: Paths Between Theory and Modern Culture*, London, Routledge.

Segal, H. (1997 [1987]) 'Silence is the real crime' in Steiner, J. (ed.) *Psychoanalysis, Literature and War, Papers 1972–1995: Hanna Segal*, London, Routledge.

Smith, P. (1992) *The Emotional Labour of Nursing: How Nurses Care*, Basingstoke, Palgrave Macmillan.

Spillius, E. (1988) *Melanie Klein Today: Vol. 1: Mainly Theory*, London, Routledge.

Steiner, J. (1993) *Psychic Retreats*, London, Routledge.

Stern, D. (1985) *The Interpersonal World of the Infant*, New York, NY, Basic Books.

Strachey, J. (ed.) (1953–1966) *Standard Edition of the Complete Psychological Works of Sigmund Freud*, 24 vols, London, The Hogarth Press and the Institute of Psycho-Analysis.

Urry, J. (2000) *Sociology Beyond Societies: Mobilities for the Twenty-First Century*, London, Routledge.

Afterword

Peter Redman

Contents

1 Attachment, detachment and the making of social worlds

As the book's Introduction argued, in exploring varied processes of attachment and detachment, the chapters that make up *Attachment: Sociology and Social Worlds* can be divided into two broad orientations: those focusing primarily on the practical *mechanisms* by which processes of attachment and detachment are achieved (Chapters 1, 3 and 4) and those focusing primarily on *emotional investment* (Chapters 2 and 5). However, as the Introduction went on to note, the chapters can also be seen as revolving a round three areas of sociological concern or debate that are referenced by the terms *mediation, matter* and the *individual* (specifically, the relationship between the individual and the social). By way of a conclusion to the book as a whole, this Afterword explores these areas of sociological concern in more detail, drawing out the various and sometimes competing ways in which they have been addressed in the course of the discussions in the previous chapters.

2 Mediation

As you may remember, mediation was defined in the Introduction to this volume as referring both to the significant role played by the mass media in contemporary social life and to the concept of 'translation': the processes by which one thing (a statement, artefact or person) is enabled 'to pass from one social world into another' (**Carter et al., 2008, Introduction, Section 2.1**). It is undoubtedly the second of these two meanings (i.e. translation) that has been most central to the preceding chapters. Nevertheless, the mass media have not been entirely absent. For example, Chapter 1 identifies the media as an important resource mediating the circulation of the beliefs, values and forms of knowledge that underpin the social meanings of childcare (see Section 4). Similarly, Chapter 4 notes advertising's increasing importance in the post-war period as a means by which consumers have been attached to brands (see Section 6). However, the most explicit engagement with the mass media in *Attachment: Sociology and Social Worlds* is to be found in Chapter 2. One of the main implications of the chapter's arguments is that people's emotional attachments to media texts actively make social worlds. Such attachments, the chapter argues, involve unconscious transference onto, or the selection and animation of, aspects of a person's habitus which are then used to 'read' or actively make sense of the text in question. As the chapter suggests, such transferences are shifting and difficult to predict in advance. Nevertheless, they serve to reproduce and sometimes modify the viewer's habitus and thus the social world in which he or she lives.

This argument also introduces the concept of mediation in its second sense, that of translation. As it suggests, from a psychoanalytic perspective, our experience of social worlds is filtered or mediated through unconscious fantasy and transference, a process that 'translates' the people and objects we find in the external world into forms that, as Nancy Chodorow puts it, 'resonate with internal experiences, preoccupations, fantasies, and senses of self-other relationships' (Chodorow, 1999, p. 14; extracted in Reading 2.1). If Chapter 2 demonstrates this argument in relation to audiences' emotional attachments to media texts, Chapter 5 applies it to relations within and between organisations and social groups. For instance, Readings 5.1 and 5.3 (Isabel Menzies Lyth's (1988 [1959]) famous study of nurse training and Margaret Rustin's (2005) commentary on the Victoria Climbié case) offer potent and disturbing examples of the ways in which unconscious anxiety, and the defences adopted against this can mediate how organisations relate (or fail to relate) to both employees and service users.

If sociological studies influenced by psychoanalysis are most likely to be concerned with the role the unconscious can be said to play in meditating our experience of the social world, it is also important to recognise that, from a psychoanalytic perspective, the social world mediates, and thereby shapes and changes, the unconscious. As the conclusion to Chapter 2 argued, the unconscious is said to come into existence *within* social meanings and practices and, via introjection, to be made and remade as an individual interacts with people and objects in the external world. The unconscious is, in this view, less a 'place' than a 'process' or 'flow' and one that is dependent on, indeed shaped and mediated by, people, objects and interactions in the external world.

While Chapters 2 and 5 provide examples of the mediating role that the unconscious can be said to play in the making and breaking of attachments, Chapters 1, 3 and 4 draw our attention to the ways in which practical mechanisms also mediate attachment and detachment processes. For example, Chapter 1 argues that, from a social constructionist point of view, women *learn* to relate to themselves as people who are 'naturally' responsible for childcare. This learning is said to occur through the medium of social meanings and the practices they organise. In other words, social meanings and practices construct women as, or 'translate' them into, people who care for children. Similarly, Chapter 3 can be understood as exploring the ways in which boxers' attachment to boxing (that is, their experience of it as being 'in the blood') is mediated by embodied social practices. In other words, from the point of view of the arguments developed in Chapter 3, individuals become boxers (persons of a particular kind) via the medium of the body-reflexive practices by which boxing becomes inculcated in them as a particular embodied disposition. Meanwhile, the various attachment and detachment devices explored in Chapter 4's discussion of economic exchange (gift tags, receipts, electronic auction mechanisms, and so forth) can all be said to mediate the precise form that a particular economic attachment or detachment takes. For instance, in the example with which the Introduction to this book began (the opening scene of the film *The Godfather*), Bonasera's attempt to buy the Godfather's services was based on the assumption that the attachment device in question (cash) would entangle him only minimally in Don Corleone's world. The Godfather's insistence that the transaction take the form of a gift translated it into a very different kind of relationship: one in which Bonasera remained in Don Corleone's debt.

The role played by bodies and material objects in Chapter 3's and Chapter 4's investigations of attachment and detachment draws our attention to a final issue that is worth discussing in relation to mediation. Just as, from a psycho-social perspective, the social is said to mediate the unconscious as well as being mediated by it, from the point of view of the 'materialist' approaches adopted in Chapters 3 and 4, the materiality of bodies and non-human objects is said to be significant in mediating (and thereby shaping and modifying) attachment and detachment processes. As the Introduction to this book suggested, this is captured, in particular, in Raewyn Connell's use of the concept of 'body-reflexive practices' (see Chapter 3, Section 5). For Connell, properties inherent to the body (for instance, Don Meredith's experience of pleasure when being anally stimulated by his sexual partner) animate social meanings and practices. In other words, for Connell, social meanings and practices are mediated by the materiality of bodies even as these bodies are mediated by social meanings and practices (Connell, 1995, pp. 56–66). As the Introduction to this volume also noted (see Section 4), although from a very different theoretical perspective, the notion of 'hybridity' found in actor-network theory (ANT) mobilises a parallel argument. For instance, as is suggested by the examples in Chapter 4, the properties of material objects, environments and technical apparatuses can be said to mediate how any given network or assemblage operates. Thus, for example, the ability of the clearing house to aggregate and settle deals in a stock exchange (see Chapter 4, Section 6) is mediated by the materiality of the recording mechanisms it utilises (whether computerised or, as was originally the case, pen, paper and ink). Without the material properties of these recording mechanisms, the clearing house would simply not be able to do its job. Acting on the social world even as they are acted on by it, the recording mechanisms are hybridised – simultaneously social and material.

3 Matter

The mediation of the social by the materiality of bodies and non-human things brings us to the second of the sociological concerns: matter. As was discussed in the Introduction to this volume, Chapters 3 and 4 can be read as being in dialogue with what they perceive to be social constructionism's failure adequately to address the extent to which attachments between people and between people and things involve materiality. Although this argument has already been explored in some detail in the book Introduction, it is perhaps worth re-emphasising a number of the issues it raises.

First, it is important to underline the fact that social constructionism does not wholly ignore questions of materiality. In particular, social constructionists do not deny the existence of a world of bodies and non-human objects; their point is simply that these do not take on *meaning* separate from the social meanings and practices with which they are entangled. To adapt an often-cited example, a rock may be, variously, a building material, a projectile, or the object of scientific analysis, but these different meanings are not inherent within the rock itself. Rather, they are *ascribed* to it via specific social meanings and practices (see Laclau and Mouffe, 1990, p. 100). Social constructionists argue that, having made this fundamental shift in perception, we are better able to see how social meanings and practices actively 'materialise' social worlds. This is evident if we return to the example at the heart of Chapter 1, that of mothers' responsibilities for childcare. From a social constructionist perspective, we can say that, in having biological femaleness ascribed to her, a woman not only learns to relate to herself as a person who has a 'natural' propensity for raising children, but, in addition, this ascription has *material* consequences. In particular, the woman concerned is more likely than her male partner both to engage in the hard work of routine childcare and to develop personally fulfilling relations with her children.

As we have seen, the theoretical positions mobilised in Chapters 3 and 4 do not disagree with these arguments per se. Rather, they suggest that sociological analysis should take into account the extent to which social meanings and practices, as well as actively making social worlds, are also *constrained* and *enabled* by the materiality of human bodies and non-human objects (Reckwitz, 2002). In other words, Chapters 3 and 4 introduce a greater sense of the consequentiality of human bodies and non-human objects than, arguably, is present in much social constructionist analysis. This, however, raises the question of the exact relationship between the material and social worlds. As the book Introduction asked, if 'materiality itself matters' does this imply that matter is more significant than the social, perhaps even constitutive of it? This is, of course, a common enough view. In everyday life, it is not unusual to think of the material world as in some sense preceding or having primacy over the social world. For example, bodies are assumed to have inherent properties that, in turn, are assumed to determine particular social outcomes (for instance, as Chapter 1 notes, men are frequently assumed to be more aggressive and less 'caring' than women and, therefore, ill-suited to childcare). However, as the book Introduction underlined, this is not the position adopted in Chapters 3 and 4. From the point of view of their respective theoretical perspectives, the social is not a by-product of the material world – an elaboration of a more fundamental material base. Instead, as was noted at the end of the preceding section, the material and the social are viewed as being present within, and constitutive of, each other.

So far in this discussion of matter and its role in the making of social worlds, we have concentrated on the debate implicit within Chapters 1, 3 and 4 and said nothing about Chapters 2 and 5. Indeed, it might be thought that, because of their emphasis on unconscious processes, materiality has very little relevance to the psychoanalytic arguments developed in these chapters. It is true that questions related to matter are far less central to the concerns of a psychoanalytically informed sociology. However, they are not entirely absent from it. In particular, the material properties of objects and people in the external world are considered to be one dimension of the factors that shape and influence unconscious fantasy and the formation of internal objects. For instance, Thomas Ogden (1992), whose work is cited on a number of occasions in Chapter 2, argues that psychological meaning in the very early stages of infancy is *primarily* organised around the experience of the physical sensation of the material world (the face against the breast, the gums, biting on a finger, and so forth), and that this material dimension of experience continues throughout life as an important strand of unconscious subjective meaning. More obviously, as Chapter 5 demonstrates, unconscious meanings can be said to shape the material fabric of the external world. Racism and other forms of ethnic hatred offer particularly stark examples of this. For instance, in Section 3, Michael Rustin suggests that hatred of this kind is characterised by paranoid-schizoid states of mind in which external others are constructed as entirely 'bad'. Extrapolating from Rustin's argument, we can suggest that paranoid-schizoid states can, on occasion, become so deep-seated that they get written into the material environment. For example, via the displacement and murder of ethnic populations, the ethnic cleansing that accompanied the wars in the former Yugoslavia during the 1990s resulted in the literal reconfiguration of whole geographical areas.

4 The individual and the social

In the Introduction to this book it was suggested that, within sociology and the social sciences more generally, it is widely accepted that individuals are shaped and influenced by the social worlds in which they live. In consequence, the Introduction noted, sociologists are less likely to ask *whether* the individual and the social are related but *how* and the consequentiality that should be accorded to each. As you will have seen, the chapters that constitute *Attachment: Sociology and Social Worlds* provide a number of answers to this question. Although with significant variations in emphasis, it can be argued that Chapters 1, 3 and 4 share a common interest in the ways in which the qualities, dispositions and capacities which individuals possess are formulated and formed by and within social processes. For example, as Chapter 4 argues, different processes of economic attachment and detachment produce different kinds of person: gift-giving produces persons who remain mutually obliged to each other; money-based transactions produce people who are 'quits'.

The strongest version of this argument is to be found in particular varieties of social constructionism which view the individual as being equipped with specific and historically contingent properties, capabilities and characteristics as they enact the social meanings and practices present within the social worlds they inhabit (see, for instance, Butler, 1990, 1993). Within such accounts it sometimes seems that the individual all but disappears. Barely more than an effect of social meanings and practices, individuals are, from this point of view, said to possess little that might be understood in terms of subjective experience or an inner world. Equally, any capacities and qualities that might be thought of as being inherent to them are viewed as few in number and of little consequence.

However, as we have seen, it is possible to argue that capacities and attributes are formulated and formed within social processes without wholly abandoning a sense of that which might be considered to be inherent to or 'on the side of' the individual. This is most obvious in Chapter 3's discussion of body-reflexive practices. In particular, as previously argued, the concept of body-reflexive practices places great emphasis on the ways in which bodies are actively shaped by social meanings and practices while at the same time being enabled and constrained by the material properties of the body. Significantly, this suggests that, in any given life course, the precise ways in which bodies and social worlds mutually interact will give rise to distinctively *individual* forms of experience.

While, compared with strong social constructionist accounts, the concept of body-reflexive practices goes some way towards reinstating a sense of the consequentiality of the individual, it is possible to argue that psychoanalytic arguments (like those adopted in Chapters 2 and 5) go further still. Most obviously, psychoanalytic accounts start from, and therefore emphasise, subjective experience in the form of unconscious fantasy and internal object relations. As a result, the individual is far more prominent in psychoanalytic arguments than it is in some competing approaches and the texture of subjective experience tends to be analysed in much greater depth. One consequence of this is that human experience tends to be accorded a greater sense of continuity in psychoanalytic accounts than is often the case in the various approaches adopted in Chapters 1, 3 and 4. As Chapter 5 demonstrated, psychoanalytic arguments view particular features of unconscious life – such as unconscious anxiety and the mental states to which it gives rise – as propensities that are liable to be present in all human affairs. In consequence, they tend to view human experience as being characterised by features that are shared across time and place. In contrast, from the point of view of the approaches adopted in Chapters 1, 3 and 4, the capacities and attributes individuals possess are thought to vary quite dramatically over time and between different places. Not only are these capacities and attributes said to change as social formations change, individuals are also said to acquire different capacities and attributes as they move from one context to another. This is because the capacities and attributes possessed by the individual are viewed as being formulated and formed within processes which are themselves historically and socially contingent.

As the preceding paragraph suggests, psychoanalytic accounts also view the individual as being endowed with *inherent* capacities – in particular, for transference, projection, introjection and unconscious fantasy. This means that they are inevitably very different from the 'strong' versions of social constructionism referred to earlier in this section. If strong versions of social constructionism view the capacities and qualities that are inherent to individuals as being few and of little consequence, approaches informed by psychoanalysis see the individual as being richly endowed with such attributes. Even when compared to the concept of body-reflexive practices which, as we have seen, accords the materiality of the body a fair degree of agency, it is arguable that psychoanalytically informed approaches go further still. In other words, the degree of agency accorded the unconscious by psychoanalytic approaches is simply greater than that accorded to the body (or, for that matter, non-human objects) in competing accounts. If this can be considered a strength, its downside is that the social is often addressed in less detail than in these competing accounts. Indeed, if in some versions of social constructionism the individual risks disappearing altogether, in some psychoanalytically informed accounts the social sometimes seems little more than an afterthought.

Nonetheless, even if too much explanatory weight can sometimes be given to the unconscious in psychoanalytically informed accounts, as the conclusion to Chapter 2 sought to argue, this does not mean that they necessarily view the unconscious as preceding the social or as somehow foundational of it. From a 'psycho-social' perspective, the unconscious and the social can be understood as being mutually constitutive or, as Chapter 2 puts this (quoting Graham Dawson, 1994, p. 51), 'abstracted levels of a single process'.

5   Concluding remarks

As both this discussion of the sociological concerns and the book's earlier chapters indicate, in investigating processes of attachment and detachment, we are not dealing with a single thing but with phenomena of varying kinds. These disparate entities and processes (for instance, internal object relations and embodied social practices) clearly work in different ways (for example, via unconscious projection and the inculcation of particular bodily dispositions) and at different levels (for instance, those of transference-countertransference; interpersonal interactions; relations within and between social organisations and groups; and those between whole social formations).

With this in mind, we should not be surprised that, in investigating different forms of attachment and detachment, we are inevitably obliged to draw on a range of theoretical resources – a fact clearly reflected in the preceding chapters. Such is the diversity involved that no single theory can encompass the different entities and processes to which the terms attachment and detachment can refer. More significantly, this heterogeneity also makes it difficult to assume in advance what the content of a given instance of attachment or detachment will be. It is for this reason that, rather than making assumptions of this kind, a number of chapters in this volume have emphasised the importance of approaching each instance of attachment and detachment as a matter for empirical investigation (see, in particular, Chapters 1 and 4).

However, despite their heterogeneity, processes of attachment and detachment have at least one thing in common. As the Introduction to this volume suggested, they are central to the phenomenon of social connectedness and, thus, to the making of social worlds. The extent to which a social world has cohesiveness, resilience and durability is due in no small part to the means by which people, and people and objects, are separated and brought together in ways that are relatively patterned, orderly and persist over time. As people, and people and objects, are configured, disassembled and reconfigured, so the contours of the social take on their familiar outline.

References

Butler, J. (1990) *Gender Trouble: Feminism and the Subversion of Identity*, London, Routledge.

Butler, J. (1993) *Bodies That Matter: On the Discursive Limits of Sex*, London, Routledge.

Carter, S., Jordan, T. and Watson, S. (2008) 'Introduction' in Carter, S. Jordan, T. and Watson, S. (eds) *Security: Sociology and Social Worlds*, Manchester, Manchester University Press/Milton Keynes, The Open University (Book 1 in this series).

Chodorow, N.J. (1999) *The Power of Feelings: Personal Meaning in Psychoanalysis, Gender, and Culture*, New Haven, CT, Yale University Press.

Connell, R.W. (1995) *Masculinities*, Cambridge, Polity Press.

Dawson, G. (1994) *Soldier Heroes: British Adventure, Empire and the Imagining of Masculinities*, London, Routledge.

Laclau, E. and Mouffe, C. (1990) 'Post-Marxism without apologies' in Laclau, E. *New Reflections on the Revolution of our Time*, London, Verso.

Ogden, T. (1992) *The Primitive Edge of Experience*, London, Karnac Books.

Menzies Lyth, I. (1988 [1959]) 'The functioning of social systems as a defence against anxiety: a report on a study of the nursing service of a general hospital' in Menzies Lyth, I. *Containing Anxiety in Institutions: Selected Essays, Volume 1*, London, Free Association Books.

Reckwitz, A. (2002) 'The status of the "material" in theories of culture: from "social structure" to "artefacts"', *Journal for the Theory of Social Behaviour*, vol. 32, no. 2, pp. 195–216.

Rustin, M. (2005) 'Conceptual analysis of critical moments in Victoria Climbié's life', *Child and Family Social Work*, vol. 10, no. 1, pp. 11–19.

Acknowledgements

Grateful acknowledgement is made to the following sources:

Cover

Photograph: Copyright © Sami Sarkis/Photographer's Choice/Getty Images;

Text

Reading 1.1: COMMERCIALIZATION OF INTIMATE LIFE by Arlie Hochschild. Copyright © 2003 by Arlie Russell Hochschild. Reprinted by permission of Georges Borchardt, Inc. on behalf of the author; *Reading 1.2:* Reproduced with permission from Beck-Gernsheim, E. (1998) 'On the way to a post-familial family: From a community of need to elective affinities', *Theory, Culture & Society*, Vol. 15 (3-4). Copyright © Theory, Culture & Society, 1998, by permission of Sage Publications Ltd; *Readings 2.1 and 2.2:* Chodorow, N. (1999*) 'The power of feelings: Personal meanings in psychoanalysis, gender, and culture'*, Yale University Press; *Reading 3.2:* Young, I.M. (2005) *On female body experience: 'Throwing like a girl' and other essays*. Oxford University Press. Copyright © 2005 by Oxford University Press, Inc; *Reading 4.2:* Zelizer, Viviana A. (2005) THE PURCHASE OF IMTIMACY. Princeton University Press. Reprinted by permission of Princeton University Press. Copyright © 2005 by Princeton University Press; *Reading 5.1:* Menzies Lyth, I. (1988) *Containing Anxiety in Institutions*, Free Association Books Ltd. Copyright © Isabel Menzies Lyth 1988; *Reading 5.2:* Segal, H. (1987) 'Silence is the real crime', *International Review of Psychoanalysis*, Vol. 14, pp. 3-12. Copyright © Institute of Psychoanalysis, London, UK; *Reading 5.3:* Rustin, M. (2005) 'Conceptual analysis of critical moments in Victoria Climbie's life', *Child and Family Social Work*, Vol. 10. Blackwell Publishing Ltd.

Figures

Figure 1: Ronald Grant Archive; *Figure 2:* Copyright © Windsor & Wiehahn/Stone/Getty Images; *Figure 3:* Copyright © Brooklyn Productions/Getty Images; *Figure 1.1:* Copyright © Bryan Mullennix/Alamy; *Figure 1.2:* Copyright © Mel Yates/Digital Vision/Getty Images; *Figure 1.3:* Copyright © Pixland/Corbis; *Figure 1.4:* Copyright © John Birdsall www.JohnBirdsall.co.uk; *Figure 1.5:* Copyright © Meeke/zefa/Corbis; *Figure 2.1(left):* Copyright © Yui Mok/PA Archives/PA Photos; *Figure 2.1 (right):* Copyright © Charlie Pycraft/All Action/EMPICS Entertainment/PA Photos; *Figure 2.2:* Copyright © Albert Bandura; *Figure 2.3:* Jean-Baptiste Greuze, A Girl with a Dead Canary, Scottish National Gallery of Modern Art; *Figure 2.4:* Courtesy of Rachel E Chodorow-Reich; *Figure 2.5:* Copyright © Andy Butterton/PA Archives/

Index

Note: Emboldened words in the index and main text indicate key words in the interactive glossary which is available for students on the DD308 *Making social worlds* course.